MW00604299

WHY YOU WERE BORN

Other books by Jerry Downs

The Present

WHY YOU WERE BORN

JERRY DOWNS

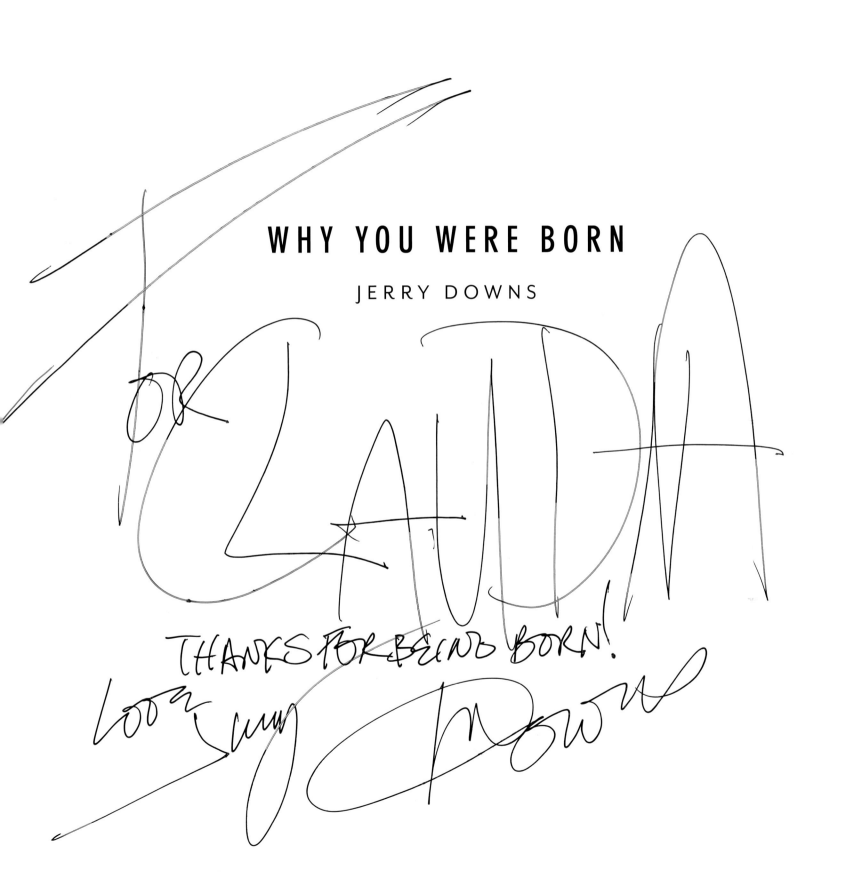

For CLAUDA

THANKS FOR BEING BORN!
Love, Jerry Downs

When I became a man
I put away childish things,
including the fear of childishness
and the desire to be very grown up.

—C.S. Lewis

Published by Jerry Downs
P.0. Box 1082
Larkspur, CA 94977
www.jerrydownsphoto.com
www.facebook.com/jerrydownsphoto
with the help of generous donations made through Kickstarter (See page 162)

Design: Michael Angelo Signorella, www.signorella.com
Publishing Consultant: Silvio Mattacchione & Co.
Print Production/Color Separation Consultant: Albert Tham/A-R Bookbuilders
Printed in Singapore, Tien Wah Press Pte. Ltd

This book is dedicated to my son, Christopher,
whose vision helped me remember…me.

INTRODUCTION

hen I was 5 years old, I made a promise. It was no pinkie swear promise. It was a blood oath. After locking myself in the bathroom, I climbed on the sink, opened the door of the mirrored medicine cabinet and pulled out my father's Gillette double edged razor. Gripping the top of the handle in one hand, I twisted the bottom of the handle to release the jaws that held the thin blue blade in place. I stopped when I realized that I hadn't thought the whole thing through.

I rewound the jaws of the razor, placed it next to the hot water knob and climbed down off the sink. Once I was on solid linoleum, I renewed the ritual from scratch. Once the blade was free, I placed it between my thumb and the forefinger of my right hand. Then, without giving it a second thought, I sliced the full length of my finger print across the forefinger of my left hand.

I had to think through the second part. Being right handed, it was harder to hold the blade in my left hand and even harder since I no longer had use of my bleeding forefinger. But I managed. My resolve was larger than anything that could ever get in my way.

Once the blade was held firmly between my thumb and the rest of my small fingers, I made an identical cut on my right forefinger. They were clean cuts with very little pain. This just wouldn't do. I placed the thumbs of both hands on the tip of each bleeding finger and opened and closed the cuts until I could feel myself start to cry. I just had to remember this. I couldn't forget. It was just too important.

Then it was time for the oath. I pressed the two forefingers together and pointed them to the sky and gripped the rest of my fingers together like you do when you pray. For a minute I let the blood from one hand bleed into the other. After I had finished counting to 60, I began to speak. To myself, to the entire universe, I made this promise: 'I, Jerry Downs,' Then I stopped. To make it more official I used my given, full, legal name. 'I, Gerard Vincent Downs, promise with all my heart, promise to find a way, when I grow up, to tell adults what they have forgotten about being a kid. I promise to find a way to remind them of why they were born.' Then, with my hands and two fingers still locked together, with my thumbs I crossed my heart and added, 'Cross my heart and hope to die.'

I felt better, knowing that my future self would help me. The helplessness subsided. There was still a lot of pain. I knew that I would still have to watch the people I loved and I knew loved me, leave from that state of unifying peace and pleasure and disappear into something that wasn't altogether human. You could watch it happen, that moment when they began to lose themselves. Their

> From without, no wonderful effect is wrought within ourselves,
> unless some interior, responding wonder meets it.
>
> —HERMAN MELVILLE

eyes changed. They smelled different. They lost touch with the surface of their body and they retreated to somewhere inside or outside of themselves. It was hard to tell which it was, both conditions could have explained the distance they had gone away.

I wasn't mad at them. It was just so sad. They knew a lot more than I did, but they had forgotten so much more. They forgot why they were even born.

I tried to tell them. We all did. "Look Mommy, look!" we yelled as we pointed to the blueness of the sky or the way light passed through a window. We took their hand and held it to our hearts and asked them to listen so that they, too, could feel how incredible it was to be alive. We tried to tell them a million gazillion times in a bazillion trillion ways.

They tried. They really did. Every once in a while, we could see them light up again, but they so rarely used the muscles required that they just couldn't hold it for very long. They just forgot. I forgot too. I knew I had to forget so that I could go through what they went through so I could write this book. I had to learn to speak their language and understand the how and why. How someone would let this happen to themselves and why, in such a perfect world, was it necessary to forget.

I forgot. I forgot so thoroughly that I came to believe that there was actually some mechanism designed to keep me from getting my hopes, dreams and desires. We all have our own horror stories. In this book, I will share a few of my own. Though there were times when I wanted to end it all, I can tell you, with all sincerity, that I would do it all again, just so I could be sitting here typing this page. I came to see that the same mechanism that gave rise to the nightmares was also the mechanism that delivered the dreams.

I could tell you why you were born right now. The answer is really rather simple. Any 2 year old could tell you. Well, maybe not in so many words. I've asked the question to a number of little kids and they usually react in one of two ways: They look at me with a look that says, "Why are you asking such a silly, self-evident question." or they do a little dance, spin around, or run around the room and joyfully look back at me to see if their demonstration answered my question. I could, also, tell you how great ice cream tastes, but words wouldn't come close to giving you the actual experience. This book was written, the pictures were chosen, to give you a taste of what it is like to remember and how important it was to forget. I

can tell you one thing: once you begin to remember, you will lick the spoon clean and ask for more. My only wish is that, by the time you finish this book, you will rip the spoon from my hand, feed yourself, and do a little dance of your own.

Still, you may be asking yourself some of the same questions that I ask myself: "Just who do you think you are? It's it a bit presumptuous, preposterous and pompous to title a book, Why You Were Born?" I've asked the first question every day of my life. It wasn't until I started showing people the first drafts of this book that the second question even occurred to me. The title came out of the same thin air, in the same voice, as everything else in this book. I forgot that it was such a big deal. Which is kind of funny. First I forgot what I knew as a child. Then I remembered and then I forgot that I forgot. The reason I can title this book, Why You Were Born, is simply because I remember and because I have every confidence that you can remember, too. I won't give you some magic number of steps to follow. I won't be telling you what to do. I hated that when I was a kid and I still don't like it. There is not one universal way to discover why you were born. There is only one way: the way you invent yourself. If you don't do it your way, it won't be yours. This book is not designed to tell you a magic formula. It's designed to foster a feeling that will help you get in touch with the answer, yourself.

You can do it. It is, in the truest sense, the most natural thing in the world. When you remember, it won't be just because it makes sense to your brain. When you remember, you will feel it with all your senses. It will be alive in every touch, taste, smell and sound. Everything you see will be a proof that you, yourself, know. You will be a part of it all and you will own it. It will be yours. It won't feel presumptuous, preposterous or pompous. It won't feel foreign. It will feel natural, familiar. It will feel like home.

This is my story. It's about how I, personally, got lost and how I found my way home. I found my way back by remembering what it felt like to be a child. You don't have to remember your childhood to remember why you were born. It was just the path I took. My own revelation came by a very circuitous and, often, painful route. Fortunately, there were moments of extreme beauty that inspired me to keep taking the next step. Along the way I took pictures, made drawings and assembled massive paper collages to record the paths I have pondered. When I began writing this book, it had nothing to do with my childhood, keeping my promise to my 5 year old self or asking why I was born. As I looked through all my pictures, I saw that they each, in their own way, were a kind self-portrait. It became clear that the different selves who took the pictures or made the works of art, were looking for something. They were looking for me, my Self. When I asked myself when I felt most like myself, the answer was clear and immediate. It was when I was a child. I remembered being full of wonder and how perfectly wonderful it felt.

You will feel your own way. Life is a work of art. And, as that Picasso guy once said, "Every act of creation is first an act of destruction." So, let it rip. I invite you to tear this book apart. Keep what is important to you, save what you think you might need for later and throw away the rest. Reassemble the pieces in a way that pleases you. This book is yours. For what ever reason, by whatever route, you found yourself here. Thank you for that. Thank you for coming to play. Let your own spirit move you. Life doesn't move along a straight and narrow path and neither will this narrative. Every image, every memory, each page is simply another expression of a time when I, personally, faced the music, took note of what rang true, discarded the dissidence, found the beat and found myself celebrating the fact that I was born.

When I was 5 years old, I couldn't believe that adults could forget something so intimate, so precious. When I made my blood oath, I knew I would forget. I did. And, I knew I would remember.

I did. What I remembered is not unique to me. We are all in this together. It's the reason we were all born.

All the answers reside within you. Listen.

nce upon a time, just before dawn, out in the country called Wheat Ridge, Colorado, I was 4 years old. The nearest neighbors were across the street and a quarter of a mile away. The neighbors, my parents, my ten brothers and sisters were all asleep or not yet born. I was awake from a dream that told me to go outside and "Just listen." Except for the stars, it was pitch black. It took a minute for my eyes to see the beginnings of blue defining the flat horizon of The Great Plains, to the East. In the West, there were distant stars, but not the outline of the Rocky Mountains, five miles away.

I ran through the alfalfa field and rested under a row of Russian Olives. I listened to my heart and then I heard the birds, just a few at first. They were Meadow Larks mostly, answering one another, together, in the dark, miles apart. It was not an alarm, just a friendly wake up call. I wondered what the words were and wished that I could whistle, just enough to say, "Good morning." A rooster crowed and the crows rose from their roost. They lit into the sky. The East was pink. The West was turning blue. The birds were now blacker than the sky. Starlings now flew where the stars had been. I could see the outline of the mountains and the trees, but not what lay beneath the black.

I closed my eyes, so that I could better hear the birds. The volume was so loud I was convinced that every leaf on every tree had turned into one of the world's hundred billion birds, each singing its own song. Perhaps it was only a million Mockingbirds. I couldn't tell more or have cared less. I was overjoyed. So transfixed was I that it was all I could do just to hold the tune. I tried to think. What were they saying that they had so much to say and so wished to be heard? Were they just trying to wake up or were they discussing their dreams, from the night before, before they disappeared?

Then my thoughts went away. My mind held only harmony. I held a note and it carried me through the trees and into thin air. The sound was everywhere. Everyone was singing all at once and then all at once it stopped. I opened my eyes and looked into the sun that had just cracked the horizon. I stared into the East, watching the Earth turn sunny-side up. I turned around to see the light of day on the scene that had held only sound. I could see everything now, a whole range of mountains, all of the trees and every single leaf. All of the birds had disappeared save a single Meadow Lark singing to someone unseen.

As a boy of four, it was no more of a mystery that the birds had turned themselves back into leaves than any other mystery I had just witnessed. Like the fact that there were birds and trees, that the sun rose and that I was there to see and hear it all. I went to feed the chickens and collect the eggs. They were still warm. I looked back at the trees and then up to the sky. It was a beautiful robin egg blue.

Innocence of eye has a quality of it's own.
It means to see as a child sees,
with freshness and acknowledgment of wonder.
It also means to see as an adult sees
who has gone full circle and once again sees
as a child, with freshness and
an even deeper sense of wonder.

—MINOR WHITE, PHOTOGRAPHER

 was the 5th of 11 children. The little boy, in the dark shirt, with his elbows on the bed is me when there were only 8 of us. That was how old I was when I made my blood oath.

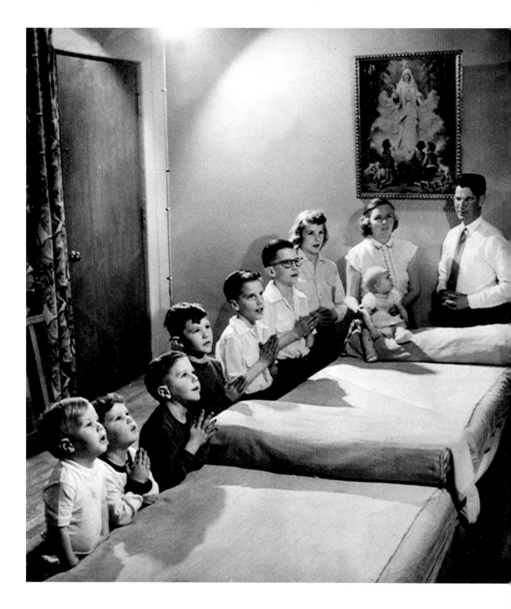

Being in the middle of a large family was very educational. There was always someone being born. There was always a toddler learning to walk, talk and hold their own. There was always a preadolescent off by themselves or a teenager learning to walk the talk and hold their own. There was always someone leaving home. It was a good introduction to the principles of evolution, relativity, parallel universes, uncertainty and chaos theory. Being the middle child, it was easy to see that everyone was connected, everyone was unique and that we all received support from the same source.

By the time I came along, the children did most of the child raising. Everyone had a role to play. From the time I was four until I was seven, my role, my talent, was to comfort the crying babies. As Newton might have observed, the household would be moving along in a state of motion and then the external force of a baby crying brought everything to a halt. The baby would cry. Everyone stopped and then, in unison, they would all say, "Jerry!," which was my call to go take care of it. There was no need for them to yell, it just made them feel better, knowing that they were doing something to solve the problem. They all knew I knew the formula.

It was really quite simple. First you check for the things that would make yourself feel uncomfortable: being hungry or having crap in your pants. Babies have different kind of cries and once you've got the language down, you can know what the problem is before you even reach the crib. The most distressing kind of cry, the one that drives parents and everyone in earshot crazy, is different. It is more emotional. It is a cry for help, a cry to be comforted, a cry for connection.

To comfort a screaming baby is a good trick. You need to know a few things to pull it off. Remember that, first and foremost, babies are kinesthetic. Touch is their first language, the one they know by heart. They just came from inside another person's body. You can't get much more kinesthetic than that.

As things get smaller, Newton's laws begin to break down. When dealing with babies you need to enter the realm of relativity. Most people pick up a screaming baby and gently rock them back and forth. All this does for the baby is say that you don't get it. You're not listening to where they are coming from. You are not connected. Listen. The cry has a rhythm: Ala, a la, AH LA, a la, a la, AH LA. Match the rhythm.

You don't shake the baby. You rock to the rhythm. Pull your arms back and forth, rock your own body in large movements. Make comforting sounds that match the volume and duration of the individual cry syncopations. 'Yes, okay, you're OKay, oh baby, BAby, baby, baby, baby.' Let them take the lead. Once your are in sync, stay there. You can, actually, feel them fall into the rhythm with you. They know you are listening. They know you understand. They trust you. From there you can slowly calm the rhythm. They will follow you until you are rocking them gently and they fall asleep or look at you glowingly, knowingly, thankfully.

One more tip: Once the baby is sound asleep they are still listening with their body. Don't just put them down. Gently put them in the crib and keep in touch. Rock the crib to the rhythm of their breathing. Gently back off until they are comfortably breathing on their own.

That's all you need to know. If you get the principle of how this works, you will know the point of this book. It is the formula for taking better pictures. It's all you need to know yourself better, make better products, better relationships, a better life, a better world.

Being the baby whisperer, also gave me another advantage over most people when it comes to remembering what it was like to be a child. I, through my younger brothers and sisters, was able to have a fresh reminder of what it was like to be a very young child. And, even though this blows my mind now, I even had access to what it was like to be a baby and remember what it was like before I was born. Again, at the time, it all seemed perfectly natural. It even had a real world, practical purpose.

Picture this: I'm 6 years old. The baby is crying and all my magic and mothering is not doing the trick. I give up and go for help, but not from my parents. I get my three younger brother and sisters. They know just what to do. Mary, the 4 year old, asks, Shawn, the 2 and a half year old, to ask Maggie, a one year old toddler, to ask the baby, Nancy, what she needs. The answer comes back through the chain of communication, "She doesn't want anything. She just fell down and scared herself. Don't pick her up. It will only distract her. She knows we're here. She'll be fine in a minute."

Though I had some memory of what they meant, I still had a crying baby. I still had people yelling, "Jerry!" from the other room. I said, "She's lying in a crib. How could she fall down?" Shawn looked and me and said, "Don't you remember anything?" Mary broke in and said, "That's how you learn to walk. You practice over there." I could tell they liked being smarter than their older brother. I asked, "Over where?" Mary answered, "Over there....where we came from." Shawn nodded his approval of the answer. Maggie was touching the baby's hand and turned around and smiled as Nancy quit crying.

I remembered. I remembered the whole thing. I remembered being over there being the Being that chose to come here. Choosing a world where I would be the middle kid in a big family. Where I would grow up in the country and go to school in the city. A world where I would learn to see physical reality from a number of points of view. I also remembered that I had forgotten and I knew I would forget again. I just wanted to cry.

I waited until I was outside and in the middle of the alfalfa field. When I was finished, I heard a sound. I popped my head up at the same time a pheasant was popping up his. This was one of my favorite things in the whole world. Every time I saw the brilliant red head of a pheasant against the bright green of the alfalfa, I felt blessed that I had been born in such a beautiful world. I stood up. The pheasant disappeared along with my fear. I watched his path by watching the alfalfa move above him. It all came back to me. I knew I wasn't alone.

Suddenly, I understood that a much larger part of myself was watching over me. I knew that Divine part made me and made the pheasant and made the pheasant pop its head up at just that moment. I, once again, felt the connection and remembered my own enthusiastic choice to be born in this exact time and space so that I could expand my own sense of self and in turn expand the larger Self that connects us all. I felt an enormous sense of gratitude to that

Self and felt that Self's gratitude for me. It was just what I needed. I wasn't alone. We were in on it together. I knew I would forget this, but in that spacious present, I fully accepted the gift. I knew I would forget, again. And, I knew I would remember, even if it took a lifetime to unwrap the present, again.

I find that for a photographer,
at least this photographer,
the element of discovery is important.
I don't repeat myself well. I want and
need that stimulus of walking forward
from one world to another.

—MARGARET BOURKE-WHITE

The thing I love most about being a photographer is that I get to see so many different worlds. When I was first starting out as a photographer, people advised me to specialize. Art directors would look at my portfolio and say, "Wow. You can shoot anything." And when a job came up to shoot a martini glass, they got a guy who shot liquor for a living. Galleries would say, "Very good work. But we have no way to market someone who takes picture of everything. You need to specialize. You need to have a style. You have no style." One gallery owner told me, "This is a great picture of a barn. You should do barns. People like barns."

It was good advice and I completely understand and even agree with what they were saying. It made perfect sense from their point of view. It just wasn't the way I viewed the world and it definitely wasn't the reason I became a photographer. It wasn't a wise decision as far as fame and fortune were concerned, but in the long run, the decision to specialize in making everything special has made me the photographer and the person I am today. Looking at things from every possible perspective, to see it in its best possible light, over time, does something to a person. It did something to me.

I like barns. I really do. And, I like being surprised by the sensuous curves of a manure shovel laying up against the side of the barn...

I also like street walkers…

and heavenly bodies…

impalas…

and birds of paradise…

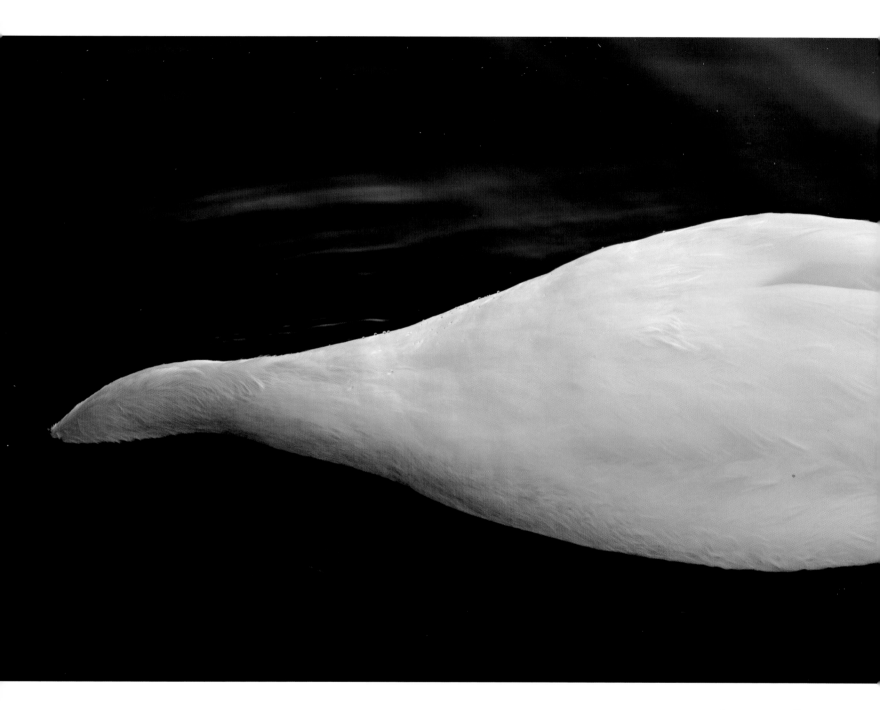

an elegant swan dive…

or making a big splash…

the world from a bug
or birds eye point of view…

mountains…   and, from time to time, a martini, too. I like, I love it all.

s a young child I was solidly grounded in a world where time and space were relative. I was a good kid, a golden child with blond hair. In a large family, if you're not crying or making trouble, they leave you alone. Being left alone, I was free to live in any world I wished. I got to be in this space much longer than most children. I even had more time there than some of my brothers and sisters. I liked being by myself. They seemed to like a different kind of interaction more than me. I always did my chores and came whenever I was called. I didn't complain. It was just logical to me. If you complained, you got screamed at and if you kept complaining you got hit and then you still had to do the work anyway. To me, that was too time consuming and no fun. I got my work done because I wanted more time to play with my brothers and sisters or to go be in my own little world.

It wasn't little to me. For years I went to this other planet and played with two lizard looking kids, a boy and a girl. We never talked in words. We played hide and seek a lot. The hide and seek trick was different than the way we play it on earth. The one who is "it" stays in one place while the other two ran and hid behind the large boulders that covered the planet. Before you ran off, everyone agrees on a single image that is different for every round. The way you found the others and the way you got caught were the same. If

When we play, we sense no limitations.
In fact, when we are playing,
we are usually unaware of ourselves.
Self-observation goes out the window.
We forget all those past lessons of life,
forget our potential foolishness,
forget ourselves.
We immerse ourselves in the act of play.
And we become free.

—LENORE TERR

someone who was hiding thought about the image, you knew they did and they knew you knew.

The two that were hiding usually worked as a team. Talking and telling jokes was one form of distraction, but more often than not, the best strategy was to do something dangerous that required your complete concentration. Jumping from the top of one rounded boulder to another or sliding down a particularly steep slope worked well.

The one who was "it" wasn't just sitting around doing nothing. In their mind they were watching the whole adventure, plus they had the added advantage to be able to see slightly into the future. So, if someone was about to get hurt, they thought the secret thought and the game would be over. We were the best of friends.

I also got to go see Carl. He was this older man who my parents knew. Every Saturday after we went to get groceries they would drop me off at his house for a few hours. Sometimes a woman answered the door. She wasn't his wife. He said that she was a caretaker. I took that to mean that she took care of things so that he could work on writing his books. We hit it off from the first time we met. We were, as my mother said, soul mates. He understood me and I, in my own way, understood him. We just talked. We talked about science and bugs, God and religion, psychology and the things that bug people. He talked to me like I was an adult and I talked to him like he was my equal.

This went on for a long time and I looked forward to it every week. One day I went to see him and he wasn't his usual self. Normally, our conversation was sparked by something that happened during the last week or just by looking at one of the hundreds of small objects that lined the window sills or half covered his large desk. I invented one game where I would run my hand over one of his many bookshelves, pull out a random book and say, "What's this one about?" He had a collection of hour glasses that told different times. I would turn over the five minute glass and say, "Go!" I took the idea from him after he said that if someone can't explain what they are talking about in five minutes, than they don't know what they are talking about.

He said that we needed to talk about something special that day. He said it with his back to me. He said it in his "I am being an adult" voice. He turned around, softened, and sat down. In his real voice he said, "Jerry, we have always been honest with each other. There is

something that I haven't told you and I've known it for a long time. I'm going to die. And, as it turns out, that time is soon. This will probably be the last time we get to see each other." He paused and, half talking to himself, added, "At least, in this world." He kept talking, something about how death is the way life refreshes itself, but I wasn't really listening to the words. I just felt the comforting tone of his voice. I just looked at this old man, my friend, and tried to take in as much and as deeply as I could.

The tone stopped. I went to him. He moved to one side and I sat next to him in his chair, the one that had lion heads on its feet. He put his arm around me and I held his hand on my lap. I had never touched his hand before, except when we shook hands as I came and left. It looked very fragile. I turned it over and saw a scar that ran across the full length of his palm. "Where did you get that?" I asked. Then he asked, in the same voice he always used to talk to me, "You want the real story or one that is make believe?"

I said, "I don't care. But don't tell me which one it is." He agreed and began the tale. "It happened when I was fishing in Turkey." I stopped him. I knew where Turkey was, he had shown me on his big globe, but I pulled on his arm, looked up at him and said, "You're just pulling my leg. You can't fish in a turkey." He started to laugh. I started to laugh. We laughed until we both cried the tears we needed to shed.

That was the last time I saw Carl. He died the following week. The funeral was going to be the following Saturday.

As I'm sure you have guessed by now, given that I had 10 brothers and sisters, our family was Catholic. Every night we said the rosary. After all the Our Fathers, Hail Marys and Glory Bes, there was another prayer. In the prayer there was a part where we prayed that some of us would become priests and sisters, a part for the conversion of Russia and a part where you prayed for those who had died and gone before us. The day I found out Carl died, I was waiting to hear his name, so I could pray for him, too.

His name was not mentioned that night or any night for the rest of the week. They knew how much he meant to me. Why, why, why didn't they say his name. Was it because he wasn't Catholic? I didn't know if he was or wasn't. He was just the most loving, caring soul I had ever met. Didn't that count for something?

Saturday came and went the way it always did. We got up. Half of us dressed ourselves in hand-me-down clothes. Whoever's turn it was, cooked bacon and eggs for breakfast. We did our chores. Somebody argued about the chores not being fair. Someone laughed out loud and everyone wanted to know what was so funny. We went to the grocery store. All the middle kids fought over who got the prize in the cereal box. The older ones didn't care and the youngest ones knew we didn't have a chance of getting it unless our mother interceded and gave it to one of us. Somebody hit somebody. Somebody got hit for hitting somebody. That day everyone, but me, went outside to play. We had pizza for dinner with crust made from Bisquick. We didn't go to Carl's funeral.

I got dressed for bed in the pajamas that I had gotten for Christmas. I had three older brothers who had grown, as all young children do, faster than the clothes wear out. The pjs were the first fresh store bought clothes I ever owned. I was beside myself with joy when I opened the present wrapped in Sunday funnies newspaper. I went to my parents room, along with the rest of the family, to say the rosary. I was beside myself with grief. After the five decades of beads passed between my fingers, it was time for the final prayer. I waited, once again, for my friend, my mentor's name to be mentioned. When it wasn't, I added, as powerfully as my choked voice could muster, "And Carl. And Carl, too!"

The rosary ended. We all made the sign of the cross and got off our knees. My mother called me over to where she and my father were sitting on the bed. She asked, in a very loving voice, "Who's Carl?"

I knew right then that they didn't know. It was just another one of those things that was happening to me, with increasing frequency, as I got older. I couldn't answer. How could the people who had brought me to his house every Saturday not know? I knew that these two people, sitting on the bed, who I loved with all my heart, didn't know because they could only live in one world. They completely forgot that they lived in many worlds. They and this specific world, were asking me to do the same. I had already stopped going to the other planet. I could never find my friends because of the tornado that began to happen each time I landed on the planet. At first, the tornado was distant and we still had time to play. It got closer every time I arrived. By the time it was over, I arrived right in the eye of the storm and couldn't see a thing.

My mother gave me a hug. My father patted me on the head. They told me to go to bed. I left the room and stood, out of view, next to the doorway. It's where we all stood when we wanted to know what my parents were, really, thinking. My father said, "God, I don't know about that one. He's just not all here, is he? I'm worried about him." Then he used the expression he used to describe people who had gone crazy. "I don't want him ending up in some room cutting out polka dots." My mother replied, "Don't worry. He'll outgrow it. They always do."

A human being is a part of a whole,
called by us, 'universe',
a part limited in time and space.
He experiences himself, his thoughts and feelings as
something separated from the rest...
a kind of optical delusion of his consciousness. This
delusion is a kind of prison for us,
restricting us to our personal desires
and to affection for a few persons nearest to us.
Our task must be to free ourselves from this prison
by widening our circle of compassion
to embrace all living creatures
and the whole of nature in its beauty.

—ALBERT EINSTEIN

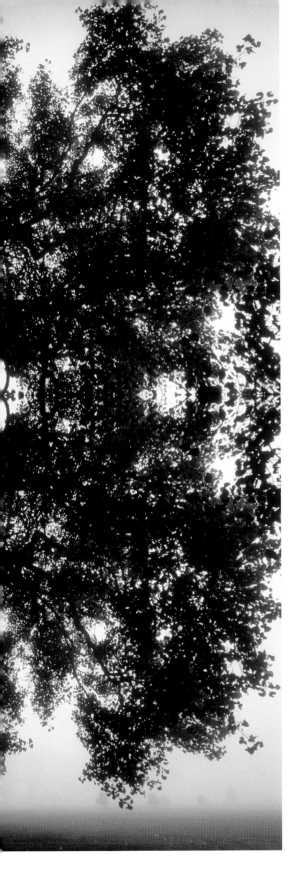

THE USELESS TREE

Tzu Ch'i of Nan-poh was traveling on the Shang mountain when he saw a large tree which astonished him very much. A thousand chariot teams could have found shelter under its shade. "What tree is this?" cried Tzu Ch'i. "Surely it must have unusually fine timber." Then, looking up, he saw that its branches were too crooked for rafters, while the trunk's irregular grain made it valueless for coffins. He tasted a leaf, but it took the skin off his lips, and its odor was so strong that it would make a man drunk for three days together. "Ah!" said Tzu Ch'i. "This tree is good for nothing, and that is how it attained this size. A wise man might well follow its example."

—A selection from The Gospel According to Zen.

 found myself in a fog one day. The picture I took and the photo-collage I created was a psychological self portrait of my current state of being. I am barely in the picture. The tree was a Rorschach that represented the spiritual and mental world in which I lived. The tree has no trunk, no roots. At the time I felt like I had so much to bring to the world, but had found no way to translate my gift in the material world. I was having trouble with "the connection."

I had become a photographer because I saw the magic in the medium, but the magic was all gone. I was on the ladder of success, but as Joseph Campbell says, it was "against the wrong wall." I was paid thousands of dollars a day creating annual reports and national advertisements, but a funny thing happens when you become "known." Ad agencies and their clients hire you because your portfolio shows a kind of innovation. They don't hire you to be innovative, they hired you to repeat that same kind of image that they saw. It was almost like they were looking in a catalogue, seeing something they liked and then saying, "Do that kind of thing with my product." They wanted certainty. Their reputation and large amounts of money were on the bottom line and so was mine. That was what I believed at the time, anyway. So, of

course, I operated from that point of view. I had plenty of grounds to support my point of view. The truth was rooted in something that ran much deeper. There was no way for me to know that then. I wanted my true path. I didn't know that the path included passing through a patch of fog.

The morning I took the self portrait I got up in the dark. I needed to get to a real estate development about 20 miles away. There was no sunrise. An unusual fog covered my region of Colorado. I knew that they wouldn't print a picture of their property in the fog, especially when they could have a choice of seeing the condos bathed in warm light as they looked out over a glowing green golf course. Who wants to live in a fog?

I got in the car, turned the heater on high, and kept my mental conversation going full speed, 'God, what's wrong with me? I should have known better. This kind of crap is always happening to me. As soon as I get ahead, something always fucks up.' You can imagine. It wasn't pretty. Then, I looked out the windshield to give the fog one final look of disgust. Then I said to myself, "God, what's wrong with me? This is fucking beautiful.' I shut up, shut off the car, got my camera bag and tripod and headed for the tree.

Visibility was less than fifty yards. I walked onto the golf course until I was invisible to human eyes. I set up the tripod, set the exposure, set the self timer, took off my clothes, tripped the timer, ran into the negative space I had composed in the camera and exposed myself to the film. I didn't feel much like Adam in Eden. I felt like an animal ill equipped to handle prolonged exposure to the environment. As I ran back and forth to the camera, taking different exposures and compositions, I began to warm up. The chill only returned when I was standing still. I began to think, 'With the proper wit and movement, I might be able to adapt to this rugged form of freedom. No, maybe not, but I am ready for a change.'

During that same month I had to reshoot two other jobs. I hadn't had to reshoot a job for years. In every case, I could be excused of any responsibility. The lab really did get the film caught in the machine. Fed-X actually lost the package. But, I could see through the excuses. I was withdrawing my energy from the whole process.

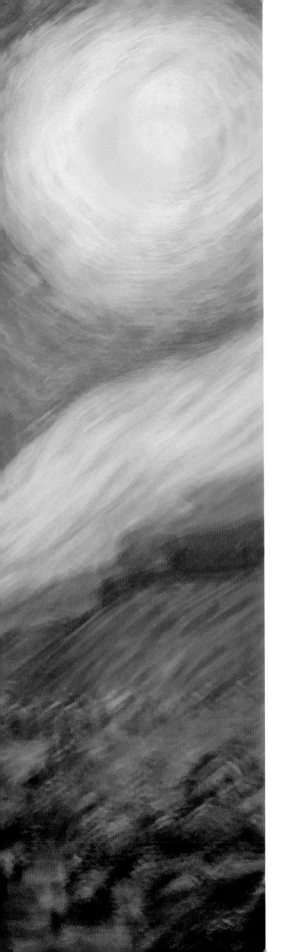

Dreams, if they're any good,
are always a little bit crazy.

—RAY CHARLES

WAKING UP IN A DREAM

At the end of that month I had a dream. In the dream I was one of seven people sitting around a conference table. Everyone else at the table was me, but the other six were me in different parallel worlds. There was no hierarchy. We were all the same, all equal in one another's eyes. We went around the table, each giving our own version of an annual report. We described what was going on in our lives and then, from the distance of our own personal perspective, gave our take on what the others were actually doing. A theme began to arise. We were all dealing with the fear that accompanies the desire to create a new life. We were caught in uncertainty. Even if you are creating a new universe you wonder if you are going to get it right. The advice was always the same, "Be present, do the best you can and let the creation have a life of its own."

When they got to me, I remember one of them saying, "There is something that you can do that you are very good at and so are a number of other people. And, there is something that you are good at that no one else is good at. In fact, no one else would even care to do it the way you do it."

Then, one of the ones that was a women added the insight that doing collages was my therapy, my mediation. She said, "When you look at all of the pieces and find a new way for them all to fit together, it helps familiarize you to the same process that will allow you to do the same thing for yourself. At least, that is the way it is for

me." Another guy, knowing full well he was speaking about us all, laughingly said, "Yes Jerry, I think we can all agree. You need a lot of therapy." We had a good laugh.

They, those other selves, as well as the other Self that we were all a part of, kept an eye on me. The very next night I had a dream where my 4 year old self was reminding me that I once used to get up before dawn so that I could hear the birds sing. I remembered that the sound was so loud. The 4 year old said, "At one time you could turn all the leaves into birds with just a thought." I got out of bed and told, my then wife, Jennifer, that I was going to the studio. I had a lot of picture books. I grabbed every one that was about birds and began to cut out the pages and sort them into groups. By the time the sun rose and set the next evening I had already cut out eight hundred eggs, three hundred of which turned into the pebbles on the beach in the collage that appears in the beginning of this book.

For the next six months I worked, 10-16 hours a day, on the six by eight foot artwork. My family and friends wondered what I was up to. Why had I given up a successful profession to cut out pieces of paper. When they looked around the studio, that was littered with thousands of pieces of paper and stacks of meticulously cut images of birds, they would ask me what it was going to look like. I could only tell them about the dream and that it had a life of its own. They understood the part about it being my therapy. I received a lot of support. For the most part, they left me alone to work it out myself.

After it was done, it took another six months before I sold the image as a poster to the San Diego Zoo, another eight months before I sold the poster to The Nature Company. I made enough to pay the rent and feed myself for another six months. Two months after that, the phone, gas and electric companies had all given me shut off notices. I had given up my studio. Every surface in my rented house, including the floor, was covered with stacks of papers, artwork and bills. During this same time, I had continued to make collages. I did it every day, needing something, anything, to tell myself that I was working, that my life was working. I questioned what I was up to and wondered if I had made the right decision to give up photography to cut out pieces of paper. I felt completely lost. I didn't know where I was going and I had no faith in the way I had gotten into this sorry state. There was nowhere to go, so I just sat down in my only chair. I couldn't even move.

I don't know how long I sat there motionless, my mind running a million miles an hour. All that running around eventually hit on a time when I had hit a similar looking wall. I remembered a time when I felt just as bad, maybe even worse. No, definitely worse. That made me feel a little better that it was worse and it made me feel worse because I had degenerated, once again, to such a hellish place.

Take a break. Turn the page. Look at some nature. Read a couple inspirational quotes. Get a bigger picture. Come back and I promise to tell you the whole sad story and it's triumphal conclusion. It's good to get lost in the story. It's, also, good to remember that it is not the only story.

I do not know what I may appear to the world;

but to myself I have been like a boy playing on the sea shore

and diverting himself and then finding a smoother pebble

or a prettier shell than ordinary,

while the greater ocean of truth lay all undiscovered before me.

—SIR ISAAC NEWTON

The only way to make sense out of change
is to plunge into it, move with it, and join the dance.

—ALAN WATTS

kay, I feel better. For a minute there, I forgot what this book was about. But, I'm happy to report, that I caught myself. I got lost in the drama, the emotional content of my past. It's easy to do. We all love the drama and it helps form a connection. "It's", as we humans are want to say, "only human." The connection is the important part. At a certain point, commiserating, doesn't help. It just makes everyone involved co-miserable. It makes the pain the important part. It's important to remember that we are not only human.

Alright, just because I promised, just for the sake of connection, just to show how I come up with a useful tool to help me through my painful childhood and all the confusion I carried with me into being an adult, I'll tell the tale of how bad it actually got. Get out your kleenex, let's dance.

I'm young, late teens, early twenties. I was doing the odd job from time to time, playing with photography when I could afford the film and, just because I felt I had to, I made collages. Not the elaborate, X-acto knife crazed versions you see in this book, just simple full frame images glued to mount board, sized and butted up one against another. They sometimes covered an entire wall in the bedrooms where I lived. I think, even then, it was a kind of therapy.

I got the images from old magazines and used books. Looking back on it now, I think I kept looking at so many different images as a way to connect to a world that I had yet to understand. As you have probably, already, and properly so, painted this picture in your mind, my life was not financially sound. That didn't help. But the soundness of my mind concerned me more.

Yes, I had a shitty childhood once I started school. But, I was never abused, never had any physical malady. In my mind, the only thing bad that happened to me happened because of who I was and how I looked at the world. Look at the image on the opposite page. It's a detail of my first large collage, titled, On Earth as it is in Heaven. Now, picture turning your head away from the book and imagine that every object is seen in just as much detail. Every object has more than one meaning. A chair is not just something you sit on and kind of disappears when you are not using it. It is the tree and the paint and the person who made the chair and the smell of sawdust on the floor of where it was made. Now, extend that same complexity to every single object in the room and imagine that all of it is seen all at once, all the time. As a four year old child, this ability was like being in Heaven. As an adult it was a living Hell. When I was by myself, I spent a lot of time just keeping the overwhelm at bay so I could make it through the day. The world wasn't the problem. It didn't do anything to me. I, myself, was the problem. Or, so I thought, and so I was.

I was alright when I was with people and was, actually, quite social. I was a good friend. I was the one who you felt free to call when you needed help moving. When I went to a party, I stayed and helped do the dishes. I opened the door for everyone, not just old ladies. If you needed someone to talk to, I would listen. It helped me stay focused, connected.

One day, when I was by myself, making the rounds to the two used book stores in town, is when it happened. I had already been to the first store. I started there because they had a free book box outside the store. So, even if I didn't have any money, I could usually walk away with something. This particular day I hit the jackpot. They had a whole lot of natural history books, with fantastic illustrations, in the free box. All of them had some sort of water damage. Some were swollen and rippled to twice their original size and others had just a few stains. I took the least stained copies and the most damaged. The rippled paged books were artworks in their own right. Their misshapen bodies each an example of the laws of physics that were written on their pages.

With my armful of books I walked to the other used book store a half a mile away, obsessing the whole way. There were dozens of ideas about what I would do with the books and my usual avalanche of thoughts. 'Where would I get the money for glue. I just ate a candy bar an hour ago, would that be enough for dinner? Look at the rust on that car. It matches the leather binding on this book. Why did that person cut off the other person turning at the stop sign. Look at the panic on both their faces. If I tore all the pages out of this book and overlaid the waves with one another, would it look like an ocean? That cat has only one white spot on it's black fur. I wonder if the origin of the word, "hide" comes from its being hidden by fur. I wonder what breed of cow this leather binding came from?' And... And... And... Thousands of thoughts per minute, multiple voices overlaying one another vying for attention.

By the time I got to the other store, I was beside myself, oscillating between the overwhelm of wonder and worry. Then I had to make up my mind about what to do with the books when I went into the bookstore. I turned the momentum of attention that I had been using to process the outside world on myself. 'I'll leave them outside. No, these are too valuable.

Someone will take them. I'll hide them in the bushes. What if someone sees me? Just go in. I know you have no receipt. You don't get a receipt if they are free. Just explain. No, no, NO. Not when I'm like this. I couldn't get the words out.' Each thought trying to out scream the other to be heard. When that didn't work, they tried inflicting pain to make their point. Each "NO, no, No, was a needle being stabbed and twisted. You get the picture. Imagine filling this page and the next and the next with random, rampant expressions of self rage that leads to this, 'What is wrong with you? I should just end this, once and for all. You really are insane. Just end it. Stop it. STOP IT! For God's sake, make it stop.'

That was it. My brain just stopped. I don't know if my brain had had a short circuit or if it was some sort of self imposed electrical shock therapy. There was nothing but silence. I stood there on the street corner. It could have been a minute or half an hour.

Then I heard a voice. It sounded like it was coming from somewhere outside myself. It was still in my head, but unlike the minute and years before my brain stopped talking, it was the only one

speaking and it was calm. It asked me a series of questions. "Jerry, if you heard someone talking to someone else the way you talk to yourself, what would you do?" "I would immediately come to their aid." I answered. Then came the next question, "Jerry, what percentage of the day are you happy and what percentage of the time are you unhappy or depressed?" "Four percent happy and 96 percent unhappy or depressed." I answered. The voice asked one last question, "Do you know what to do?" In a single, calm voice I answered, "Yes...yes, I do."

And I did, too. I didn't go into the book store. I went home, put down the books in one of the few remaining clear spots on the floor and I sat down to take it all in. I was so enjoying the quiet that I didn't turn on the radio or TV. I didn't put on a record. I didn't do any of the things I habitually did to distract or calm myself down. A single thought came. I contemplated it. Paused, and let the next one float to the surface.

My brain came knocking. I told it I was busy and to come back later. I was having a conversation with myself and I was enjoying the company.

We didn't come up with a plan of attack to fight off the beast. We found a way to comfort and feed the starving creature. The plan was simple and only included 2 steps: 1.) Every day, at the end of the day, I would ask myself what percentage of the day was I happy and what percentage of the day was I unhappy or depressed. 2.) When I found myself afraid to do something, I would ask for help. If I didn't want to do the dishes, I would ask my other self, the one that would do anything for anyone if he would help. If I didn't want to answer the phone because I feared it was a debt collector, I would let him answer it. He loved the arrangement and I did, too.

This may sound like some sort of Schizophrenic episode. Perhaps it was. For me though, it was a vast improvement going from hundreds of voices to just two.

Now, go back to me, twenty years later, back before I made you take a beauty break, to me sitting comatose in a chair, feeling terrible that "I had, once again, degenerated to such a hellish place." I only had remembered the pain and completely forgot the cure. My situation, my circumstances, were still the same....."the phone, gas and electric companies had all given me shut off notices. I had given up my studio. Every surface in my rented house, including the floor, was covered with stacks of papers, artwork and bills."

I asked for help. The voice said, 'What do you need?' I answered, "I need to find my way out of here." "Perfect," the voice said, "Let's start with what is right in front of you. The desk. How about we start with the desk?" My mind interjected, "But, but, but, how will I find anything. I know where everything is." "Oh really?" the voice chimed in, "You know where everything is but you don't know what to do with it. You are so overwhelmed in how big the "problem" is that you can't see why you should even bother to pick up a single piece of paper." It was hard to argue with the voice. It knew me too well. We took all the papers, notes, pictures and bills from the surface of the 3x8 foot foldout table that I used for a desk, and unceremoniously dumped them in a box.

"God, that is fantastic." We said in unison. "Now what?" I said and excitedly added, "Never mind. I know exactly what I want to do next. Let's go clean the mirror in the bathroom!" Again, we said in the same voice, "Great idea! There is not a single space in the whole house that looks better clean than the surface of a mirror. It makes the whole room look cleaner." And we were right. We polished that baby until it gleamed. I barely looked into the mirror during the cleansing ceremony. I just concentrated on the spots of toothpaste, dust and soap until not a single spot or piece of lint from the paper towel was visible. We stepped back and took a good look at our fine work and, for the first time, I took a good look at myself. I wasn't looking at how my hair looked or my day old beard or the spots on my skin. I was looking at what it looked like to see myself completely and utterly happy.

"Wonderful, what's next?" I said to the person standing right in front of me. "Let's clean the sink and then the toilet, Yeah, the toilet would be fun. Clean away all the shit. What a great metaphor. Then we can go back to the big floor and maybe even vacuum as we clean a spot and then…." "Wait a minute…. Wait a minute. Who let you in?" I said to my brain. "You did." The kind voice and the brain answered in unison. I took a deep breath to collect myself and said, "You're right…. You're right. You are what's next. I know I can't do this without you. I know…. I know I told you all those things to tell me. I've been giving you mixed messages my whole life. I know…. I know that every time you told me what I told you to tell me that I started screaming at you to stop. But we have to come up with something else. If you want a body to be in, we have to change. I can't take it anymore. I won't take it anymore."

They didn't say a word. It was if they were actually listening to me. That simple gesture touched me very deeply and gave me the courage to continue. "Okay, let's start here. Forget about the toilet. Forget about the house. Let's take a walk and we can talk." We stepped out of the bathroom, stepped over the piles of paper on the living room floor, looked back at the clean desk, and walked out the door into the clean air of a beautiful Summer afternoon.

I still saw everything, all at once. But, nothing had or needed a story. The sky wasn't an accumulation of atmosphere that was acting as a prism reflecting the blue spectrum of a ray of light that had been on the surface of the sun eight and a half minutes before. It was just the sky. I didn't even see it as blue. Nothing had a name. It just was. And what it was, was wonderful. There were still a hundred billion things acting as themselves with their own individual integrity, but there was no hard edge. Everything was connected. Not because one part fit into another part and then that fit into another for infinity. The connection was not mechanical or mental or scientific or religious. It was not a metaphor. It was more like an emotion. Everything was connected because everything was the same thing, just a different expression of the same thing. Not like we were all drops in the ocean and we make up the ocean. We were water itself. Sometimes a solid. Sometimes a liquid. Sometimes a gas. Each was just a different expression of the Something more basic and pervasive then can be personified or given a name.

There is no release without a little grease.
Nothing sublime without a little slime.

—AUTHOR UNKNOWN

It wasn't like things were shutting down or getting narrower. Without all the noise, I was free to feel the breeze, notice that I was in a body, be. We didn't need to talk. We just needed to feel like this as much as we possibly could. We all knew we would forget. We all knew we would, if asked, go through the whole thing again, just to be here, again. It wasn't foreign. It was familiar. It was home. I saw that I wasn't my story. I wasn't the artwork. I wasn't the pieces of paper on a floor. They were all just expression of me. I was me.

I took it all in. I took in all I could let in. I took in all I could stand. I went home, took a bath and went to bed. I knew that I wouldn't, couldn't, shouldn't live in that space forever. I knew that tomorrow I would, could, should pick the next thing in front of me and continue. And, and this is a pretty big "and", for the fist time in years, the percentage of time I was happy and the percentage of time that I was unhappy or depressed had begun to shift.

The next day the sky was blue. That was good enough. My fears rose their head again, but they were not as ferocious. I had help. The part of me that liked to help, helped me stack all the papers on the floor into piles. I did, as my brain suggested, clean the toilet and vacuum the floor. With each completion, I felt a little better. Every time I looked at all I had to do, I got depressed. Every time I got depressed, I heard a gentle voice reminding me to just do the next thing in front of me. It found ways, with the help of my brain, to recall times when I had successfully faced something so impossible. The bird collage leaned against the wall behind another fold out table covered in stacks of paper. The frog collage on the opposite page, and half a dozen others were stacked against another wall. When I moved them to vacuum the floor, I was reminded that each one was the completion of something impossibly complex and time consuming. I remembered that the same rule I learned while creating a collage also applied to cleaning the room or reclaiming my life. Just pick up the next piece of paper, see where it goes and if it doesn't go somewhere, put it away for later or throw it away.

When I started to go through the box of papers that I, and my new found friend, had filled with the piles of paper on my desk, I came across a 3x5 print of me, naked, in the fog. The next piece of paper, stapled to the back by that former self, was a xerox copy of the Useless Tree story. I thanked him for facing his fear. I thanked the selves who appeared in my dream and the 4 year old me for reminding me that there was no separation between us, that everything was

connected and that all I had to do was believe it into being real. I thanked the largest part of me for turning water into a gaseous state so thick that it hid the sunrise and the blue sky on that pivotal day. I put the print and the piece of paper in a box that contained ideas that I might use in a book, someday.

Halfway through sorting the box, the phone rang. I answered it all by myself. It was someone from a publication I had never heard of, Bird Talk Magazine. They had seen the poster of the bird collage that I had done for The San Diego Zoo and wondered if I was selling the poster without the zoo's logo. I was. The weight of a thousand of them was over in a corner pressing Fall leaves that I had gathered a few months before. The person on the phone thought the poster would be perfect to put in their Christmas gift ideas section. The listing was free. I thought their terms for inclusion fit my current business model. I agreed. She thanked me and I thanked her. I hung up the phone, looked to the sky, and thanked God. I put the paper with their information on it in the "Important" pile. I took the next piece of paper out of the box and put it where it belonged. Admittedly, I was a little distracted but, by this time, the sorting no longer required my full attention. I tried not to start counting my chickens before they hatched. I tried to keep my mind on what I was doing. My mind said, "It's okay to dream. It's good to picture this turning out well. Enjoy it." I could even talk to myself now. I added, "Yes, it's true, isn't it. I don't know what the future will bring."

How could I? I've never been there before. Then I added, to everyone involved, "As we all know, when we are fearful or uncertain, it always turns for the worse and when we imagine a positive outcome, it can turn out any number of ways and we, at least, haven't destroyed our life in the time it takes to get there." Now that I had to answer to myself every night before I went to bed, I was finding new ways to keep the happy percentage of my day growing.

Orders began to come in November. It payed the rent and the utilities and payed my brother, Jimmy, back the money I borrowed to keep the lights on, the month before. I filled the orders and along with each print I included a thank you note and one of the thousands of exotic bird feathers that I had gathered over the years. I got a kick out of imagining them opening the tube and having a beautiful feather fall out.

About mid-December I got another call. It was from Toronto, Canada. My first thought was about my son, Christopher, who was with me every weekend, sticking a pin on the map we had set up to show where all the posters were going. The man, Silvio Mattachoine, who later became my good friend and who contacts me every November 13 so we can wish one another a Happy Birthday, said that he wanted two posters. One poster for himself and one for a friend of his who had a small personal aviary with some very large parrots and macaws. I sent out the posters and in about a week he called again. Silvio said his friend loved it and wanted to know if the original was still available and if I had any more originals for sale. I glanced around the walls of my now clean room, smiled to myself, and said, "Yes, it is and yes, I do."

Silvio didn't promise anything and he let drop that his friend loved to collect wildlife art and that he had a great deal of "disposable income." I called my friend Joe, who I'd been taking road trips with, off and on for the last twenty years, and asked him if he wanted to drive 3,000 miles to Canada and back to Colorado in the middle of the winter. It didn't take him a minute to answer. In early January, Joe flew to Colorado from California and in the middle of the night, in the middle of a snow storm, in a rented Ryder truck, we hit the road.

As always, our conversations spanned events from our past, our hopes for the future, things we had read and the nature of the universe. Before we reached the Colorado/Nebraska border, the nature of our immediate universe included snow falling so hard that you couldn't see another car coming until it was in your headlights. For whoever was driving, it was important, if we wanted to stay on the road, that we be very present. The road had to be read. Snow on concrete behaved differently on black top. There was the kind of thawed snow that refroze with an icy surface. Then there was the kind of wet snow that picked up the truck as we hydroplaned our way to Toronto. It was easy to see how Eskimos or Inuit, as they like to be called, could have more than fifty words for "snow." Like Inuit finding their way to the hunting grounds by feeling the currents change in the bottom of their kayak, we were driving by the seat of our pants.

What lies behind us
and what lies ahead of us
are tiny matters compared to
what lives within us.

—HENRY DAVID THOREAU

We stopped to take pictures and for gas and that was it. We ate in the truck and drove straight through, taking turns sleeping in the back or staying awake talking to keep the other awake while they drove. By the time of this road trip we had already driven together thousands of miles and covered a lot of territory in our shared exploration of life. From the first time Joe and I met, we were the best of friends. We both grew up in the country. Though, Joe laughs when I say that. I grew up, twenty miles from downtown Denver on three acres with no animals. As my father would say, "Sure, we raise animals. We have 11 kids." That always got a big laugh from the adults and a lot of eye rolling from the kids.

Joe grew up on a cattle ranch in South Dakota where the nearest town, of any size, was thirty miles away. He had one sister who was 4 years younger than himself. I went to grade school in the city and he went to grade school in a one-room school house. He was the only person in his grade all 8 years. For me school was a kind of nightmare of overwhelming information. By the time Joe was in 4th grade, he had already heard the classes of all the grades above him a number of times. To give himself something to do, he read the Encyclopedia Britannica. Some things were different, but we both lived on a dirt road, we both knew how remarkably beautiful it was to see the red head of a ring-necked pheasant pop up in a field of green alfalfa, and we both knew how to drive in the snow.

We made it across the border, met Silvio, had our first sit down warm meal and went to see the collector. Joe and I unloaded the half a dozen artworks one at a time. We crossed the Katakaqtanaq covered (hard crust snow that gives way underfoot) parking lot, carried them through the lobby and up a flight of winding stairs. After all the trips, we took off our coats, unwrapped each piece and placed them around his large office. I liked the collector right away. He was a real regular guy, casually dressed in a flannel shirt, blue jeans and cowboy boots. He may have been a regular guy but, to my relief, he was also more than a little eccentric. He, who had started his hardware/software business in a garage not 10 years before, proudly showed us around his plant.

After taking the full tour, with stops to see a section he had enclosed for his collection of exotic orchids and to meet the rather large and loud parrots and macaws, we sat down and started talking turkey about price. His opening price for the bird collage was more money than I had made in the last three years. I replied, "I don't think so. That wouldn't even pay me a minimum wage for the work. This piece took me six months, working at least 12 hours every day. It took more than a mile's worth of cutting with an X-acto knife to cut out every one of those pieces of paper. And the gluing, that was the hardest part." We went back and forth. After a time, it was clear that he was going through all this for the fun of it. He bought the bird collage, titled, Birds of a Feather and the piece called, On Earth as it is in Heaven. He paid $20,000 for each piece in US dollars. He also said that he wanted to buy the remaining pieces over time and wanted to commissioned me to do one on horses. As a gesture of good faith, he gave me an additional $10,000 to get me started on the horse collage.

Joe and I were riding pretty high on our way back to Colorado. He was happy for me and I was walking around in a dream come true. I do remember taking the northern route and stopping in South Dakota to see his parents. I do remember stopping for gas and sitting in various truck stops and splurging on warm, sit down meals. And, I absolutely, with no equivocation, remember driving the empty Ryder truck, at night, the full length of Wyoming in the wind. This is not the Grand Teton, Yellowstone Wyoming. This is the deserted flat plains of Eastern Wyoming. There's not much out there. One time I had a photography assignment on the Wyoming/ Montana border. The client and the owner of the mine I was going to shoot, was also a pilot. From the height of the Cessna, there were periods when I didn't see a town or a farmhouse or even a road for over half an hour, several different times. From that height it looks perfectly flat, but from ground level, it kind of rolls.

The crest of each wave is probably only 50 feet high. The top of each undulation was spaced under a mile one time and over five the next. For an interstate highway engineer, I'm sure, this just didn't make the grade. When the highway was built, they cut though the high spots and used the dirt to fill in the low spots, so the road, itself, is pretty flat. I'm sure, on a nice day, this made driving much more pleasant. Things change when you add a little wind.

As the locals like to tell you, Wyoming ranks first in the US in average annual wind speed, and they are damn proud of it. One joke they tell tourist is that Wyoming is so windy because Utah blows and Nebraska sucks. It's just local pride talking about Utah and Nevada, but when it comes to the wind they are completely correct. As Google will tell you, "During the winter in Wyoming, there are frequent periods when the wind reaches 30 to 40 mph with gusts of 50 or 60 mph."

The wind wasn't too bad when we stopped to fill the thermos at a truck stop in Buffalo. By the time we came out the mood had changed. We saw two men straightening out a tarp on the top of their 18 wheeler and knew that Wyoming was about to have one of her frequent periods. There was nothing to do, but go with the flow.

At that time of month there was no moon. There was no snow either. It had all been blown away. The road was clear. It was my turn to drive. There was a door behind the seats to the cab of the truck. I waited until Joe got through the door and settled into the make shift bed before I shifted into first and set out down the road. I loaded my travel cup with coffee and set the thermos bottle in a place that was easy to reach when I wanted a refill. For the next four hours I didn't have another cup. I couldn't because I couldn't take my hands off the wheel. Ten minutes didn't go by until the wind was wailing against the side of the large, empty truck I was driving. I needed both hands and a knee against the wheel to hold the 14x8 foot box on the road. It was like driving a kite. Then, all of a sudden, the wind almost stopped and shifted directions. I had been correcting the wheel against the wind so hard for so long that I almost ran off the road. Almost, just as quickly, the wind returned and I was, once again, over correcting to meet the changing circumstance. The situation was so dangerous, the night so dark, that I focused on the road with all my might. Then it happened again. The howling wind was reduced to a loud whisper and then, again, just as suddenly, the wheels would wobble and the truck would rock wildly back and forth as I frantically tried to right the situation.

I didn't need coffee. My body was mainlining adrenaline. My forearm muscles ached from pulling so hard against the steering wheel. I needed to calm down. There was no way I could continue my current approach much longer. I asked for help. "Take a breath. Now let it go. Now, look further down the road." That was all I heard and all I needed. With a wider perspective I could see the source of why this was happening to me. I could see it coming. The wind had been being blocked by the 50 foot high walls from the cutout of the high spot in the hills and it returned with force as soon as I had passed the walls. I had been so focused on the road that it had been invisible to me. The wind didn't stop and the cutouts continued for another hundred miles. The only difference was, and this was a big difference, I could see them coming and knew when they were about to end. The truck rocked back and forth with the same force, but I knew it would. And, this is a very big 'and,' it had happened enough times that I no longer feared that the truck would tip over. I let myself see further down the road. I knew the wind would eventually end. I knew that I would make it.

We made it back to Boulder and I began to make plans about what I would do with all the money I was going to make for the rest of my life. I brought Joe to the airport and made him an offer to come back to Boulder and we would write the book we had talked about for years. Then I went home, sat in the chair that I was comatose in three months before, in front of the same desk that I and my new found self had cleaned and wrote over $30,000 in checks to pay my bills and pay back all the people who had lent me money. I had about $12,000 left. I was the richest man in the world.

My life was laid out in a straight line before me. I rented a new studio in Coal Creek Canyon, in the mountains above Boulder. I immediately began the horse collage. Joe came and we began to work on a book. The two sided 6x6', A Horse is a Horse collage, took eight months to complete. When I was six months into it, my collector benefactor, had a glitch in his software/hardware product and had to recall so many pieces that he couldn't buy the remaining pieces, couldn't buy the 5,000 horses, couldn't afford the orchids, closed his plant and he was the only soul left in his building except for the large and loud parrots and macaws. I guess he, like myself, couldn't hold the success. Given that I had given up the idea that anything happened TO me, I had, of course, had to draw the conclusion that this event was my own creation. Somehow, I had engineered the whole thing. I had laid out a path, removed all the hills and filled in the valleys and was blown away when conditions changed. I had become so focused on the road in front of me that I couldn't see the long view. I never saw it coming.

I wasn't happy about it, but it didn't destroy me, either. I asked myself, "What's wrong with me?" But I caught myself saying it. Having been in such a repetitive series of ups and downs, I did think it would be a good idea to examine the story I was telling myself. It was, I had to admit, nothing new. But knowing that didn't scare me the way it once did. When I was younger, there were times that I thought if something didn't work out I would die from the embarrassment of the failure. I remember what a revelation it was to me that I kept not dying. Yes, it stung me, but it didn't stab me in the heart. It shook me pretty hard, but it didn't blow me over. I was still alive and I knew that I was the one driving.

I continued down the road. I knew, somehow, I would make it. After finishing the horse collage, I began to write a book that was never published. Some of which I rewrote for my first book, THE PRESENT, and some of the ideas appear in the pages of this book, as well. I still saw my son, Christopher, every weekend. I was still kind and loving to his mother, my still good friend, Jennifer. All my friends stayed in my life. I was connected to something larger than my circumstances. Perhaps, it was from that space, my next artwork was the World of Worlds collage that you saw at the beginning of the book. Joe, who had come for a time to work on a book together, was now back in California. We discovered that, even though we thought alike, we don't express ourselves the same. He was still my best friend and the phone still worked, so we could talk from time to time. As I tell you to this all now, it is just a story. Fortunately, at the time it was happening, I could tell myself, that, at some point in the future, all that I was going through would be just that, a story.

> # Live your life as an Exclamation rather than an Explanation.
>
> —ISAAC NEWTON

can, I could, tell the story any way I wished. I could tell you that I had to sell my camera body and I had to give the landlord one of my large collages to pay for the four months of past due rent when I finally moved out. I could just as easily say that I had everything I needed to keep a roof over my head and continue moving forward.

The story could concentrate on how cold it was that winter, how I had to forage for wood in the snow so that I could heat the ice cold house. Or, I could describe in beautiful and romanticized prose how pleasant it was to sit at my desk embraced by the warmth of the wood burning potbelly stove, as I wrote about the wonders of the universe while watching snow caress the forest in a blanket of snow. I could focus on not being able to give my son everything I wanted to or I could relay the delight of the adventures we created, in the given circumstance, to keep each other entertained.

One of our particular favorites was born out of not having enough money for gas. From the top of the mountain where we lived, we would get the car up to speed and then put it in neutral and see if we could make it to the bottom without using the gas or the brake. It's pretty much all down hill. There is a 2,000 foot drop over the 12 mile winding road. It took a number of tries to make it all the way. There are a couple of spots that kind of level off and the car would almost come to a stop, unless, of course, you had a good head of steam when you reached them. All the way down we talked to the car. We encouraged it. "Go baby, go. You can do it. Oh yeah, that's good. Good job. Good job!" Once we made it down off the mountain there was a mile long stretch that begins with a dip and then flattens off into a gentle slope to the highway. That was more

of a trick. The last big slope out of the mountains was on a particularly tight curve. There couldn't be any cars in front of you because you have to move into the oncoming lane in order to make a wide enough turn to safely keep enough speed. Once, we made it all the way down, up the dip, all the way across the flat, through a green light at the highway and coasted to a stop on the side of the road another 100 feet. It was amazing! High fives and joyful fist pumps with resounding cries of, "YES! YES! YES! We just couldn't believe it. That light was always red. We agreed that it must have been our pure, powerful intention that made the light turn green just when we needed it.

That was pretty exciting and very educational in explaining Newton's Three Laws of Motion: Every object in a state of uniform motion tends to remain in that state of motion unless an external force is applied to it. The acceleration of a body is parallel and directly proportional to the net force acting on the body. For every action there is an equal and opposite reaction. All the rules of physics apply to the rest of life. I could use the fact that I lost my imagined future to hold me down or propel me. I could choose to react against it or let it pass right through me. My only job was to notice the resistance to past loss or my future success and see where I wanted to put my energy.

There is also an emotional kind of physics. Both apply when you are a child whose mass is so much smaller than that of an adult. Children look up to adults and adults look down at children. I remember being asked what I wanted to be when I grew up. The question had to be explained to me after I answered, "Me." The question implied that I wasn't something already. It said that a child only turned into a person when they grew up into one. I asked them, "When do you become an adult?" They gave me those catch- all phases that grown ups use when they don't know the answer, "You wouldn't understand. You are just a kid. You will understand when you grow up."

When my parents found out about my imaginary friend, Carl,

my mother comforted my father with the phrase, "Don't worry. He'll grow out of it." I knew I had given Carl up to "grow up." I saw that it was important to be like the others if you wanted to be with the others. It wasn't the only thing I gave up. When my mother told my father about it, her tone wasn't comforting. It was laced with fear.

I was four, maybe even younger. Mommy was telling my older sister Eileen that she was going into town the next day, so she had to be there to watch the kids. I casually reminded her, "You are not going tomorrow. You have to be here when the repairman comes to fix the refrigerator handle." "What do you mean? Did someone break the handle?" she asked. "No, not yet. Jimmy (my next oldest brother) doesn't break it until this afternoon." I answered wondering why she didn't know, herself. She was busy and dismissed what I said and told me to go outside and play. I obeyed.

And, of course, Jimmy swung on the handle and it broke off. We couldn't get in to get food. Jimmy was feeling a little unloved and separate from his part and importance in the family and needed some attention. My mother was worried about him. My father was worried about money and feeding the kids. So to satisfy what everyone was feeling, Jimmy broke the handle on the refrigerator door. What was so hard about that?!

After calling my father at work and saying over the phone, "I know. I know. But we still have to eat." After she looked "Refrigerator Repair" in the Yellow Pages. After she made the call and said, "Not until tomorrow? Ok, I'll see you tomorrow afternoon." Not until then, did I see her look at me. Not until that moment had I ever seen that look directed at me. To me, her darling Jerry, she said, "How did you know." How did I know? How does anybody know? Doesn't everybody know? Not knowing what to say, I said, "I don't know." She snapped, "Well, don't ever do it again!" I obeyed.

My mother was only partially right when she said I would, "outgrow it." I did and I didn't. I was born in November, so I could have started first grade when I was five, about to turn six or six about to turn seven. My mother kept me home for the extra year because, as she told my father, "He's just not ready." and because, as she told me, "I didn't want to give you up. You were just such a joy to have around and you were so helpful with the babies." I remember just the two of us being together in that last year before starting school. My father was at work. The older kids were in school and the young-er kids were all taking a nap. I remember her in a dress. She never wore pants. At the time it just wasn't "lady-like." I remember her sitting on the stairs and me sitting on her lap and saying, "Do rock a bye baby." She would say, "You're too old for that." I would smile and say, "No, I'm not!"

Rocking me like a baby, she began to sing, "Rock-a-bye baby, in the treetop. When the wind blows, the cradle will rock. When the bough breaks, the cradle will fall and down will come baby," Then she would speed up the words really fast, pull her knees apart and while she sang, "cradle and all," I would fall and she would catch me in her dress. I was getting too big for the full effect of the fall, but it wasn't about that at all. It was something that was just between the two of us. We must have done this a hundred times. It always ended the same way. We would kiss and then we would hug. I would say, "I love you, Mommy." and she would say, "I love you, Jerry." This was why I chose to stay in this world and let go of all the others. I stayed for love.

> The mind is a fire to be kindled, not a vessel to be filled.
>
> —PLUTARCH

s the crow flies, Holy Family Grade School was only 5 miles away. As a six year old child who had only known the country it was another world. My father would drop the kids off on his way to work and they would take the bus home. My first grade class had too many children, so I only went to school half a day. This meant that I had to take the bus home by myself. My mother took me on a trial run two days before school began. We walked to the bus stop which was a mile away from home. I did the same walk many times with my brothers and sisters. That's where a small country store was that sold penny candy. I'm sure they sold other things, but the bins next to the cash register is about all I remember. They also sold candy bars and Cracker-Jacks with a prize inside, but they cost a nickel.

I'd never been on a bus or been anywhere away from home with just my mommy. I was excited and terrified. My mother handed me a dime before we got on the bus. Once we climbed the steps she showed me the box next to the driver. She told me to hand the dime to the driver and say, "Change please." The smiling driver took the dime and put it into a slot at the top of a changer that was attached to his belt. Then he clicked the changer two times and handed me two nickels. "Now put one of the nickels in the box." My mother instructed. I did and we sat down. I took the side of the bench next to the window. She explained to me that every morning Daddy would give me a dime. I would ask the driver to "Change please." and I could go to the

store and get some candy so I had the strength to walk home where I could fix myself some lunch. She asked me if I understood. I nodded my head yes. I was used to only understanding half of what adults were talking about. It took me two months before I said to the driver, "Change please." He was such a nice man. I was afraid that he might think that I was asking him to change who he was. I saw him every day and we became good friends and one day I told him the story. He had a good laugh and began to drop me off at the store instead of the official bus stop a couple of blocks away. By the time he dropped me off that far out into the country, more often than not, we were the only two people on the bus.

As my mother and I got closer to Denver, the bus got fuller and the houses got closer and closer together. I thought it was kind of cruel that people had to live like that. We got off the bus and thanked the driver, and then walked to the school that was about half a mile away. It was orientation day. I was told where to sit. The nun, Sister Mary Something, laid down the rules about how she expected us to behave. It was quite the shock. The day before this, I was being caught in my mother's skirt as she sang Rock-a-bye-baby and was playing hide and go seek with ring-necked pheasants through rows of corn and suddenly I was in a row of desks being tossed kernels of information by a ring-necked nun. I just wanted to hide and have no one ever find me.

After the orientation, my mother and I walked back to and waited at the bus stop. She explained that I had to be at the bus stop before 12:20. "School gets out at 12:00. That should be plenty of time for you to get here. If you miss the bus, you will have to wait another hour for the next one to arrive." Again, she asked if I understood and, again I nodded my head yes. I wasn't talking much, except to myself. I was having a hard time taking in so much information.

We got on the bus. My mother paid a dime for her and a nickel for me and we sat down. Then, not more than a minute later, as we were driving past Lakeside Amusement Park, I saw something that changed my life forever and for the better. On the far end of the huge parking lot a group of men were setting up a huge tent. Then, from out of a big truck with big colorful letters on the side, a man led an elephant. "Look, Mommy. Look!" I screamed. There, right before me, was a real live elephant! I had seen one in a book and tried to draw it with Crayons, but they actually existed in real life, on this very planet. I only saw it for a few seconds as the bus rolled on. It was hard to imagine why we weren't all stopping to take a better look. Suddenly, I had an overwhelming sense of relief. Yes, this new world held all kinds of scary things, but it also had elephants! Years later, while I was listening to a video about the history of the United States, I learned that in the 1800s, when people were asked why they were going West, they often offered this reply, "I'm going to see the elephant!" Which was to say, "I'm going to see something that I have never seen."

The rest of the bus ride home was a joy. I opened myself up to see all that I had never seen in my whole life. After stopping at the country store to get a candy bar, we walked the mile home with me talking a mile a minute about all that I had seen.

I talked about how Lakeside Amusement Park must be the most magical place in the world. I recounted, to her great amusement, how great it was when, every Fourth of July, we all got on roof of our family's home to watch the firework display put on above the park. I said that I could hardly wait until I got older so I could see fireworks up close. And I said, "Remember when Uncle Shawn took us there? It was so much fun!" Uncle Shawn was my mother's brother who lived in Boston. He was a priest. Every summer he would take his vacation and visit us in Colorado. He was a great guy. Quite progressive, in his own way. He advocated marriage for priests and priesthood for women. He said women were just as good as men in God's eyes. He said that being a celibate priest was so lonely. He even hid the Barrigan Brothers, two pacifist priest who spoke a out against the Viet Nam War, from the FBI. That all took courage, but taking all of us kids to an amusement park, that was brave!

I loved it, we all did. We rarely went anywhere, as a family, that cost money. We savored the experience for all it was worth. I went on every ride with the little kids and even a few where I was an inch shorter than the clown that you had to be bigger than to get on the ride. We worked out a strategy. My mother would stay with the little kids while Uncle Shawn and the five oldest kids would all enter together. I stood in the middle of the group while he distracted the ticket taker. I knew it must be alright. For God's sake, he was a priest.

He said that some rules were made to be broken. We stayed until the park closed.

On the way home almost everyone fell asleep. I looked out into the darkness, replaying the entire evening. When we got home, I pretended I was asleep so that I wouldn't have to carry my exhausted body to bed. Uncle Shawn carried me in, helped me put on my pajamas and put me into bed. The next day, like every day he was there, he went to a church to say Mass. This was part of his practice and it was a way to practice the sermons he would give when he went home. Some of the littler kids went with him just so there would be someone in the pews. That day, my sister Mary and I were the only ones awake enough to go. On the way there I confessed to him that I had pretended to fall asleep. He said he knew and thanked me for being so honest.

Mary and I stayed awake the whole Mass and the long, to us anyway, sermon. The sermon was about sacrifice and Saint Simeon, an ascetic who lived in Syria around 400 AD. He lived in a cave and wore hair shirts for a few years, but thought that he wasn't suffering enough, so he built a sixty foot tower where he spent the last thirty-six years of his life. He stayed on top of the tower in an iron enclosure that didn't permit him to sit. He ate only the foulest desert roots that his followers would throw up. Uncle Shawn didn't go into this much detail, but the idea was that we should admire this guy because of his devotion to God.

On the way home Uncle Shawn asked how I liked the sermon. I said, "It was stupid." He wanted to know more. "Oh, really, how come?" "He was dumb." I said. "Okay, what made him dumb?" At the time this was happening, I was still visiting my friend, Carl. Carl was the only one I talked with about these kinds of things. He would keep asking me questions until he understood what I meant. Uncle Shawn reminded me of him, so I decided to answer his question in the same way I would answer my mentor and good friend, Carl. "Well," I started, God is love, right?" "Right." he agreed." Saint Simeon wasn't loving. He was selfish. He only did all that suffering so he could get a better seat next to God in heaven. If he was loving he would have gotten off his tower, taken off the hair shirt and found a way to help someone. He would be loving." To which Uncle Shawn said, "That is very good. I see your point. He thanked me for being honest. I thanked him, again, for taking us to Lakeside Amusement Park.

I was young then. I was a little hard on Saint Simeon. I had only

begun to learn how hard it can be to see how to love in this world. I had yet to meet the many people, including myself, who spent years sacrificing, with that same sense of self abuse, thinking it would bring me to the Golden Gate. I remember coming to this realization when I was on a road trip with my friend, Joe. We were driving up the coast from LA to San Francisco. As we traveled north from the City of Angeles, I was telling him about the lives of the saints as we traveled through a litany of their namesakes, Santa Barbara, Santa Maria, San Luis Obispo. As the sun was going down we arrived at San Simeon

and the gates of Hearst Castle, the monumental former private home of newspaper magnate William Randolph Hearst. The castle has 56 bedrooms, 61 bathrooms, 19 sitting rooms, 127 acres of gardens, indoor and outdoor swimming pools, tennis courts, a movie theater, an airfield and, at the time Hearst lived there, the world's largest private zoo. We wondered, given their sense of excess, if St. Simeon and William Randolph Hearst were the same Being in parallel worlds.

And the day came when the risk to remain tight in a bud was more painful than the risk to blossom.

—ANAÏS NIN

hen I entered the world of first grade it was not entirely unfamiliar. I don't remember learning much in our mornings worth of work, but I do remember that the best part of it was taken up with going to mass everyday. It wasn't the mass I knew going to church every Sunday with my family. Except for the teachers and the priest, everyone else in the church was a child ranging in age from first to eighth grade with the smallest children in the front pews. We all sang the mass in Gregorian chant. I wasn't too good at reading the square notes, but I knew the tune. The sound of the wall of children's voices behind and around me absolutely transfixed me back into the most sacred and connected place I knew as a young child. In one way, it was even better. I was standing on this earth using my earthly voice, singing with all my heart and floating away into the infinite at the same time. I was part of it and it was a part of me. It was divine.

The walk to the bus stop, the ride and walking a mile home from school, once I got used to it, once I didn't die from the fear and overwhelm, was quite empowering. I was on my own, doing something that only big kids and grownups did. I always made the bus even though I continually stopped along the way looking at things I had never seen before. I knew lots of different crops and exotic looking weeds but was unfamiliar with and delighted by all the trees and flowers that had been planted simply to be ornamental. Where I lived, there were mostly the native cottonwoods growing along the irrigation ditches or the hardy willows and Russian olives planted as windbreaks between the fields. Fall in these city neighborhoods was kaleidoscopic. There were Chinese maple leaves that were as red as a pheasant's head. Some kind of yellow leaves that were as big as my own head. When the wind blew and the leaves fell, it was raining flakes of a rainbow. Every day I collected the most remarkable specimens, carefully pressing them between the covers of my school books. When I got home I showed my mother the new specimens that I had discovered from my trip into that exotic frontier.

Winter was just as wonderful. I began to see the similarities of my two worlds. The fur coats on the city dogs was thicker just like it was on the horses and cows in the country. Frost clung to a chain link fence the same way it did to barbed wire. My mile long walk home from the bus stop sometimes was a challenge, but there was always something fascinating to spark my imagination and warm the part of me that was so full of wonder.

When any of us kids would complain about how hard something was, my father would tell us about how he had to walk a mile home from school. He would go on, at some length, about how he had to walk barefoot so he wouldn't wear out his shoes and how he had to hunt squirrels for food because his family was so poor. Once, when I was older, I told him how much I enjoyed my long

I had only seen roses when my father brought one home for my mother. And here were dozens of them on a single bush.

There were purple bearded irises that smelled like Welch's Grape Jelly. There were purple lilac bushes that you could smell before you saw them. They were my favorite. I would just stand there taking in as much of their loveliness as I could stand. I believed that with every breath I took in, their beauty was filling me with beauty and making me a more beautiful person.

Once, I was taking a clump of lilacs from a bush that was as big as an elephant and a woman with a pair of big scissors looked over the fence and said, "What are you doing?" She scared me. I answered, "I wanted to bring them to my mother. They are her favorites. I'm sorry. I'm so sorry." She softened and said, "That's okay. They are my favorites too. That's why I grew them." I looked down at the scissors pointed at me. She saw me and pointed the scissors towards the ground and added, "That's why I'm out here, to cut some of my own to put in the house. Here, let me get you some to take to your mother." I was nearly in tears. This might have been the first encounter I ever had with an adult stranger. She wasn't strange at all. I took the arm full of lilac branches and thanked her. She said I was a good boy and told me to take as many as I wanted for as long as they lasted. I gave one branch to my friend Eddie, the bus driver, and the rest to my mother.

When I told her the story, she said that the woman who gave me the flowers was a nice lady. She added that I should be respectful of other people's property and then we cut the ends off the stems and put the flowers in vases around the Blessed Mother statue that was in the corner of the kitchen counter. We both leaned in to smell the lilacs one more time. The blue of the Blessed Mother's burka was beautiful with the the purple flowers. What made it even more perfect was that May was the month of Mary.

walk home. He, immediately, responded, "Oh me, too. I got to take off those stupid shoes and run through the country pretending I was an Indian. When I snuck up on a squirrel, I pretended it was a buffalo." When he saw the look on my face and in his own mind remembered what he used to tell us, he added. "Hey, we all do what we have to do to get through. You try raising 11 kids." I laughed. We both laughed. We both got to remember a time in our lives when we were very happy.

And then there was Spring! Spring was like how good it feels when you have been outside in the cold for hours and you come home and and feel the warmth when you open the door. You feel happy you got so cold just to feel that good. Again, the city neighborhoods, filled my senses with new forms of fauna. First came the crocuses popping out of a late snow. Then the parades of tulips in more colors than there are in a crayon box. Then everything! Roses.

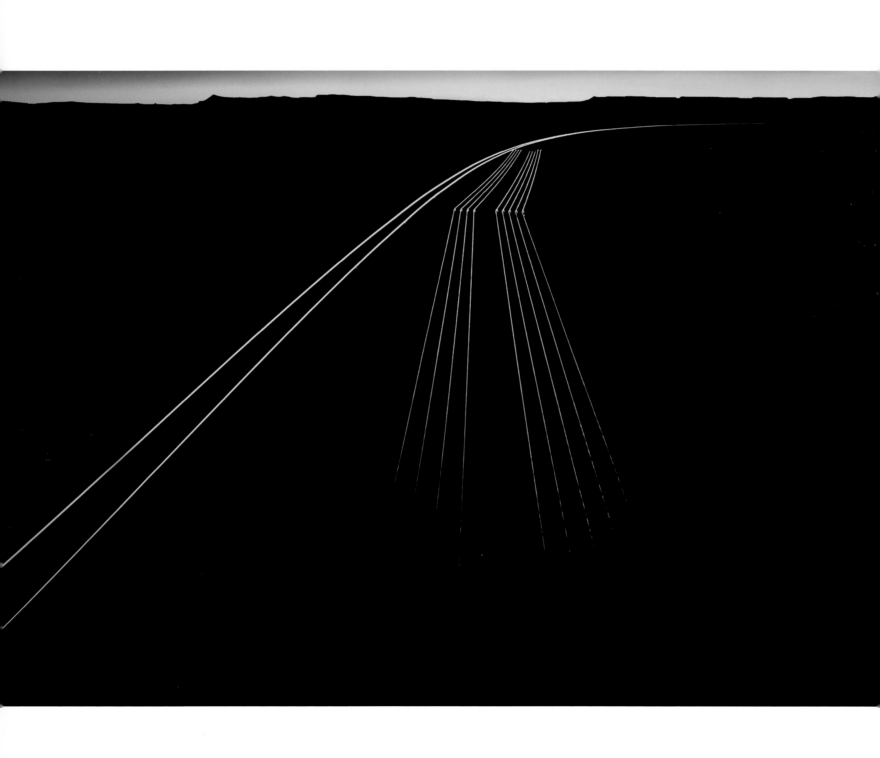

Summer came. I did what I always did. I took my shoes off. It always took a couple of weeks before my shoe softened soles were tough enough to take running through the fields. You needed shoes for somethings, of course, like walking the railroad tracks that ran along the border of our land. Steel tracks get really hot in the Summer heat, way hotter than the air. I thought it was weird that they also were colder than the air at night. It was only after the sunset, just before dark, when they were the perfect temperature for bare feet.

The train came by twice a day, going one way and then back. It had boxcars full of barley and hops that it was taking to Coors brewery in Golden about five miles away at the foot of the mountains. It also had tank cars that carried corn syrup to the Jolly Rancher Candy Company about a mile down the track.

Every evening, all summer long, around five o'clock, if the wind was right, we could smell what kind of hard candy had been made that day. The smell of cinnamon was easy to tell and we would all say, "They made Fire Sticks today." Grape and Apple always were more iffy, always dividing the kids into two camps, each certain of their own opinion.

Every time the train came, someone would yell, "Train's coming." Then we would all run out and wave at the engineer and pump our arms up and down to get him to blow the whistle. The tracks were the source of a lot of our playtime and family mythology. There was the 'see how long you could walk and keep your balance without falling off' game. Once, I walked all the way to Jolly Rancher, but no one believed me because I didn't have a witness.

That particular Summer a game of high finance got played out on the tracks. We never got an allowance. Everything belonged to the family. Even when we went to work, until the time we left home, we signed our paycheck and handed it to our father. We had to ask for every penny. When we were going to school we would line up after breakfast to get our milk money from our father. Milk was 3 cents. If you got a nickel one day, he gave you a penny the next. When people asked my mother how they could afford such a big family, she always said, "God always finds a way." We only got our own money from saving our milk money or by doing some extra chore. One summer my mother made the mistake of saying that she would give us a penny for every fly we killed. After a morning of paying out kids with handfuls of dead flies she changed it to a penny for ten. We ALL said that was unfair. Although I do admit we cheated a little bit by leaving the screen door ajar.

I only tell you this to give you an idea of how high the stakes were in this particular game we played on the railroad tracks. My brother Jimmy, the next one older than me, said he wanted to show me a trick. We went out on the tracks and he put a penny on one of the rails. After the time of, "A train's coming" came and went we went and looked. The penny was flattened to twice its size and Lincoln, barely visible, had a very fat face. That was so cool. Joey the next oldest brother and Johnny the oldest brother both heard about it and said, "Big deal. We did that a long time ago." Jimmy, wanting to gain back his stature, put a nickel on the next day.

Next, Joey put on a dime. The game was on big time now. A dime! Of course, Johnny had to put on a quarter. A quarter, you know what you can buy for a quarter? A coke, a bag of chips and a candy bar. Yikes! Jimmy was out. The stakes were way too rich for his blood and his pocket. He had to join the ranks of the little kids. It was now between Johnny and Joey. They knew it and we reminded them of it every day. Days went by. As much as they hoped we would, we didn't forget. It was no skin off our teeth and it was a great way to let them know that they weren't so big. Talk was cheap.

> To see is itself a creative operation, requiring an effort.
>
> Everything that we see in our daily life more or less distorted by acquired habits,
>
> and this is perhaps more evident in an age like ours when the cinema,
>
> poster, and magazines present us every day with the flood of ready-made images
>
> which are to the eye what prejudices are to the mind. The effort needed to see things without
>
> distortion takes something very like courage.
>
> —HENRI MATISSE 1950

After a week, side bets of a penny were placed on who would go first. Now we all had some skin in the game. Even Johnny and Joey had a bet on who would go next. One of them had to do it.

Two days later, Joey, the one I had my money on, pulled me to the side and said, "Here's two cents. Go out and wait for the train. When you hear it coming, come into the house screaming, "The train is coming. The train is coming." And then mysteriously added, "I'll take care of the rest." I went and waited.

I kept an eye peeled. I put my ear on the track. I waited. I put my hand in my pocket and played with the two pennies and the cat eye marbles that were rolling around in there and waited. Then, almost a mile away, I saw it coming. Running as fast as I could, I started screaming, knowing that someone, maybe Joey, would hear me through the screen door and open windows before I reached the house. They did. Joey and everyone else came running out. He had the 50 cent coin high in the air. And kept saying "This is it. This is it." Everyone, including Johnny ran towards the tracks. Joey stopped short and said, stay here and act like normal. We don't need the engineer seeing a bunch of kids on the tracks. As he ran the last 20 feet, he pulled the gum he had already prepared, bit off a piece, put it on the back of the coin to keep it from falling off, placed it on the track and casually walked back to the whole family. Even the babies were there. I held the oldest one and Mary held another. We were all in place way before the train was a quarter of a mile away. The coin gleamed on the track. The train came. We all waved and pumped our arms. The whistle blew. Thirty cars rolled by as we kept our eye glued to the spot on the track. The caboose passed and Joey screamed, "Not yet, Not yet! Don't let the guy in the caboose see you!" We all obeyed. He paid for it. This was his show.

After the eternity of a minute and a train load of protesting, he finally said, "Okay. Now!" We all took off and surrounded the spot in awe. Joey had stayed behind just to get a good look at everyone's faces. He slowly walked up to the track and entered the circle. He took one long look at everyone's stupefied face, bent over, picked up the huge coin, put it between his thumb and forefinger and raised a smashed silver dollar up to eye level, looked Johnny in the eye, and said "I win."

Johnny shook Joey's hand and said, "I guess I owe you a Coke." Then he started to laugh and added, "I can't believe you did that!" Joey laughed and said, "Can't believe it either!" That was Johnny and that was Joey. That was our family, the summer before I started second grade.

That was exciting. I haven't thought about that in years. You may be asking yourself, "How does he remember all this stuff?" Well, besides the things I've already explained about the advantage of being surrounded by little kids the entire time I was growing up, there are other ways I can recall it all. I always remembered more than most people. I had a whole set of stock stories. They were all self-referential and emotionally charged. But, a funny thing happened when I started to write this book. All those stories weren't just being looked at as a way to address some hurt or to bring up on a first date to show how sensitive I was, they were looked at to serve, in some symbolic way, the purpose of this book. They were stories that would help remind me and you, the reader, of what it was like to be

a kid. There was some separation. The stories I remembered, suddenly, had more depth, more detail. And, each one of those reminded me of another.

It was like looking at a movie. Like a movie, it was easy to identify with the characters, feel their joys and pain, but I somehow understood that it was, indeed, it's just a movie. I could push the "Play" button, hit "Pause" or "Rewind" or even "Eject." To get the projector rolling on the The High Stakes on the Railroad Tracks movie, that you just read, I programed in a search. I wanted something light and sentimental with enough drama to keep it interesting and fun. I thought about when I was happy. I remembered how happy I was when summer came and I could take off my shoes. Then I played one of my favorite childhood games. I played pretend. I just walked out the back screen door of my childhood home, saw the tracks and

just sat back and watched the movie. Every once in a while, I hit the "pause" button to write it all down.

It was a revelation when I realized what I was doing as I edited the story. It was the same thing that I had been doing my whole life. I was cherry picking the parts of the story that supported the plot that I wanted to tell. Using the same story, I could just as easily have written about how deprived we were and how the whole world was plotting against me, a member of a poor family who lived next to the railroad tracks. It was an epiphany to realized that the way I remembered my childhood memories had been written, produced, directed and edited by me. I asked myself, "Is that what really happened or am I just making it all up?" And the answer was, "yes." Yes, it really happened and, yes, I made up my mind about its meaning and chose the frames that I wanted to feature.

> *Miracles are a retelling in small letters of the very same story which is written across the whole world in letters too large for some of us to see.*
>
> —C.S. Lewis

The mental movie I wrote about being in second grade, I replayed, without a single edit or rewrite, for about the first 40 years of my life. In the opening scene I am sitting in my alphabetically assigned seat. By this time, I had made friends with my ABCs. "I could even sing the ABC song. ABCDEFG, HIJK, LMNOP, QRS, TUV, W, X, Y and Z. Now I know my ABCs. Tell me what you think of me." I had practiced over the Summer and even tried to sound out words under the picture books we had at home.

All the nuns were named Sister Mary…something. I don't remember to which saint my new teacher subscribed. We'll just call her, Sister Mary Jane. We said the morning prayer and the pledge of allegiance to the United States of America and to the Republic for which it stands and then sat down and folded our hands on our desks. I had seen her in the halls when I was in first grade. She had been teaching older students, but this year, because there were so many children, she had been assigned to teach the newly added second grade class. As we were about to find out, we were far behind from where we should be because we only had half a day of schooling in first grade. She was the one sent into rectify the problem. She was all business.

She began, "There will be homework every night. Every one of you are behind where you need to be to make it to second grade. You are only here because we have too many kids in this school. You need to pay attention. We will catch up. If you do as you are told you will be able to make it to third grade. If you do not, I will see you again, right here, next year." For emphasis, she hit the desk with her long wooden pointer. Then slapping the blackboard with the pointer, said, "Get out your three ringed binder and copy the words on the board on the first page and do the math problems, too." Now, I couldn't tell you what the words said. I couldn't have told you then. I couldn't read.

I began to draw the words. I loved to draw. It was my favorite pastime. It was what set me apart, what made me valuable. I proceeded to use the same approach I used to draw a horse or a bird. First I would imagine what it was like to be the thing that I was drawing. By this time, I had become familiar with the individual characteristics of each character. "A" was very important, it was like my oldest sister, Eileen. "A" was important, but she never abused her authority. "B" was a round boy. "C" was the one who had an edge, adding a crispness to the conversation. "C" could be both a boy and a girl. It was like a magpie. Boy and girl magpies both look the same and "C" made the same caw, caw as the beautiful black and white bird. Those were easy. I was still learning about the others. I knew "S" was super important. It was like the infinity sign. It could make more of everything just by being next to the word(s). But, I still had big questions about "Q." Why did "Q" always need "U" next to him? Was it lonely or did he just like his/her company?

There were also numbers on the board, something called a "math problem." They were a lot more complicated. Each one had a different value. This was a foreign concept for me. I knew everything had its own integrity but, in my world every thing was equal in value. Each blade of alfalfa in a 100 acre field were all different but the each had the same value. My brothers and sisters were all completely different from one another, my parents were different from one another, but we all were, as my mother said, equal in the eyes of God. Sometimes, the differences between the big and the little kids conflicted and I, being the middle child, acted as mediator for both camps. I didn't take sides. I just tried to find what as fair for everybody. It was always better if you let the parties, themselves, decide. Like having a candy bar and it needs to be shared by two

> The most important reason for going from one place to another is to see that's in between.

—Norman Juster, The Phantom Tollbooth

people. It's simple. One gets to make the cut and the other person gets to choose. Other situations were more complex. Say you have two scoops of ice cream left in the carton that needs to be divided between three kids. The solution is more psychological and requires a recontextualization of context. Don't use bowls. Use cups. When I handed it to them I didn't say, "This is all there is and this is all you're going to get." I'd say, "There's not enough to save. You can have it all!" As an added touch, I'd add, "Is this too much? Can you eat it all?" When everyone feels equal, the need for conflict diminishes.

To be sure, I was a little obsessive. I went through a period when I started on a different step every time I walked down the stairs, just to keep things even. I'm so pleased that I was never labeled and drugged out of my compulsions. I didn't need to be cured of any malady, I needed to master them, one step at a time.

To me, everything was alive, everything was divine, so why wouldn't this be true for letters and numbers, too. When I went to do a simple math problem, say $7 - 4 = ?$, I had to talk to all the parties involved. The 7, who was about to be diminished, the 4 that was doing the diminishing and the resulting three. The 3 and the 4 had to agree that, at sometime in the future, they would combine again and make the 7 whole again. It made sense to me. I thought all the other kids were doing the same thing. I just thought, because they had been doing it longer than me that they were on better terms with these particular beings.

This, as you might imagine, slowed down the process considerably. That day and for all the months that followed, time always ran out before I had time to get all my numbers in a row or had time to dot the "i's" and cross the "t's." When I got the hang of how the letters put themselves together to make words, I was very impressed. It was, for me, quite magical. But, when it was my turn to stand up and read I almost always got sick to my stomach. I knew that the teacher just wanted to hear how the words were written. She didn't want to know what the words were trying to say. It felt like I was being rude to the words, knowing what they had gone through to get themselves together.

As best I could, I worked out a strategy to help me get through my turn. Each child, beginning with the first child in the first row, would read one sentence, then the second one the next and so on. I would count the number of seats and then count down to the sentence I would have to read and then practice the words and explain to them that I needed their help. The problem was that if a child got a word wrong, they would have to sit down and the next person would say the same sentence. I would have to scramble to get to the new sentence and start all over again. This required a great deal of concentration, so much so that, sometimes, when it was my turn and I would read the wrong sentence because I had lost track of what the rest of the class was doing. The children would all laugh. After a while, the other kids thought I was doing it on purpose, after all, how could anyone be so stupid. They thought I was doing it to be funny or to get back at our mean teacher. I couldn't compete with the other kids academically, but I could make them laugh. I took the gift I was given and became the class clown. Sister Mary Jane was not amused.

She only hit my knuckles with the ruler on rare occasions. Her favorite form of punishment was to call me to the front of the class and have me draw a circle on the chalk board where she would have me put my nose. The length of time I had to spent looking at the blank blackboard ranged from five minutes to over an hour, depending, at least it seemed to me, on how loud the children had laughed. Other than that, I was a pretty good kid. I never held it against her.

One day, while the children were all working, I saw her longingly look out the window at a tree that was in its full Fall foliage. I finished my work, took out a piece of paper and drew the tree, the window and her looking. We handed in our work, got our book bags, and my classmates left the room. I stayed behind watching her erase the chalk board with a wet sponge. I liked the way the grayish blackboard would return to a solid black and how at a certain point, as it dried, it became exactly the same tone as her black habit. When she turned around she kind of jumped when she saw me. She let go of the reverie she was in and said in her usual voice, "Yes, Mr. Downs, what is it?" I handed her the drawing and said, "I like that tree, too." She looked at the drawing. Looked out the window. Looked back at me with kind of an embarrassed smile, the kind you see on a little kid. After a moment, which seemed like an eternity to her as she replayed what she was thinking about when she was looking at the tree, she said in the voice of the young woman she once was, "Yes, it is really quite beautiful." I went to catch the bus

with my three older brothers. I knew they would be waiting for me. I knew they would tell me to hurry up and to stop looking at things. I knew that they always wanted to know what I was looking at. It all seemed fair.

I liked religion class. Though I thought, like most things that adults talked about, that it held a lot of contradictions. But as my mother and St. Ambrose famously said, "When in Rome, do as the Romans do." I was in the Roman Catholic Church. I was also only eight years old. I practiced their customs, but my God was mine. And besides, for the most part, all you had to do in religion class was

> ## What is hell? I maintain that it is the suffering of being unable to love.
>
> —FYODOR DOSTOYEVSKY, THE BROTHERS KARAMAZOV

listen and answer questions about what you thought was right and wrong. I enjoyed looking at the subtleties of what made something good bad and something bad good.

One day, Sister Mary Jane, said, "Now I know that some people think that what I'm about to say shouldn't be said, anymore. But, it was taught to me when I was your age and I still think it is true." She said this like she was about to give us a piece of information that would save us from eternal damnation. She said, "You should only play with Catholic children. The reason we don't want you to play with Protestants and Jews is because they are not as pure and will only lead you away from the true faith. They will lead you to sin. They will lead you to hell." She summarized the point in the same way it had been summarized for her when she was a child, "If you play with dirt, it will rub off."

Now, I knew my Catechism and I also knew what I knew. I raised my hand. When I spoke I wasn't being the class clown or someone who was trying to make her look bad. I was an innocent kid, who didn't know any better, who wanted to help her see that the idea she had been living with all her life was itself a sin, a kind of blasphemy. I was sure she would want to know.

In answer to my raised hand, she said, "Yes, Mr. Downs, is there something you would like to say?" "Yes, Sister." I answered knowing that you only answer the question that you are being asked. "Okay, what is it?" "Well," I began, "what you just said, doesn't make any sense." "Oh, and how would you know, this?" she asked. I answered, "Because, it is in the Catechism." "Okay, Mr. Downs, please tell me and the class what is in the Catechism." Finally, I had the right question. I began, "The very first question is, 'What is God?' The answer is, 'God is Love.' The second question is, 'Where is God?' The answer is, 'God is everywhere.'" "So?" she said. I answered, "So if God is Love and God is everywhere than love and God have to be in Protestants and Jews and even in the dirt." I added that last part because I really liked dirt.

She, Sister Mary Jane, didn't say a thing for a long time. The room went quiet. Every eye in the room was upon her. She spoke,

"Clearly, Mr. Downs, you are confused about what I was saying. Perhaps you will understand when you grow up."

I sat down. I was very confused. Why didn't she see such simple logic? I thought about it for a long time. Then I had an epiphany. I raised my hand and waited until she called on me again, "Yes, Mr. Downs, what is it, now?" "I got it." I replied. "What did you get?" She patiently replied. I proudly answered, "God is even in our confusion."

This was huge! My sense of "everything" just took a quantum leap. I was mankind, learning that stars were not just light shining thorough holes in a big dome, they were suns. I was mankind learning that not all the stars were stars, some were galaxies. Not only did everything include every thing and every person, animal, plant, star and galaxy, it also included every concept, every notion, every idea, every thought! This revelation explained a lot. I didn't have to understand or believe everything I was told or taught. There were no absolutes in the same way that there had been a minute before. Sister Mary Jane wasn't right or wrong and I wasn't either. We just held two different ways to hold the infinite number of ways to hold the infinite. This was such a relief.

Suddenly, such notions of an angry God who would punish you if you didn't love Him in a certain way, was out the window. I never really believed it, never even thought of God as a He, but now I didn't have to give the Roman God or his Hell a second thought. Perhaps this had me so greatly concerned because we were going over the Roman Catholic ideas of venial sins, like telling a white lie and mortal sins, like murder, eating meat on Friday or committing adultery. I kept asking what adultery was, because I didn't want to go to hell because I had done it by mistake. "You'll find out when you grow up." wasn't good enough of an answer. Too much was at stake.

Hell, as the good Sister told us, was a terrible place. "Imagine," she said, "what a burn feels like. Not just a sunburn or burning your hand on a hot stove, no, it's worse than that, a lot worse! Your whole body is on fire and inside your body, too. And, it never, ever stops." To clarify what "never ever" meant, she continued. "Imagine a bird landing on a sea shore. The bird picks up a single grain of sand and then the bird flies to the farthest star and drops it off and then the bird comes back and does it again. Imagine that the bird does this to every grain of sand on the beach and every beach in the whole world. Imagine how long that would take. Now imagine that you are on fire this whole time. That's nothing! Your pain from committing a mortal sin will go on longer than that. It will go on forever and it never, ever stops." As if she she needed to, she added, "All the while you will be stabbed and cut with shards of broken glass." It seemed a little severe that a God who had created a bird and all the stars would get so upset because you ate a piece of bacon on a Friday.

Sister Mary Jane didn't seem to treat me the same way after my epiphany. She didn't call on me when I raised my hand and she asked me to stand and read more often than the other kids. She said I had to learn to read. She told me I was the worst reader in the whole second grade, maybe in all the second grades in the whole world. I wanted to get back in her good graces. The day after All Souls Day, which comes after Halloween, she told us about indulgences. There were two types, simple and plenary. They were ways that we could help the poor souls in purgatory. Purgatory was just like hell, except you could get out once you paid enough penance for all your venial sins. Then you could go to heaven and be happy with God forever and ever. The added benefit was that the poor souls in purgatory would be so grateful to you for saving them so much pain that they would put in a good word for you when they were talking to God.

Popes and bishops could give plenary indulgences that would send a soul straight to heaven, but we, simple second graders, could say an ejaculation, a short phase and it would take time off a poor soul's sentence. You could say, "Jesus, Mary and Joseph" or "Oh, suffering Jesus, Oh sorrowful Mary" and it would take ten days of pain away. I wondered if this meant that it was for one poor soul or if the ten days would be applied to everyone and just put in a pool and everybody got off a few seconds. I wondered if only people who believe in Hell or Purgatory would go there. I didn't bother to ask. I was too excited. We were going to have an ejaculation contest between us and the other second grade and I was going to prove to Sister Mary Jane that I was a good boy.

A big paper chart was put up next to the cloak room. There were lots of lines, divided into two columns, one for the boys and one for the girls. Each night Sister Mary Jane totaled the number of ejaculations. The first day's total was 156 for the girls and 200 for the boys. All of the points in the boy column were mine. The other boys said that this was just for sissies, just for girls. But, after I had received a lot of praise and the boys were now in the lead, they all started to ejaculate, too. It was between the boys and the girls. It was between the two second grade classes. It was clear, after about the first week that it was also between Sister Mary Jane and her second grade counterpart, Sister Mary Alice. I wasn't doing it for the poor souls. I doubted that they even existed. If they did, I would let their Roman God figure out how to divide the payoff. I needed to win for our team. I needed to win for our class, for the boys and for Sister Mary Jane. I needed to be good at something.

Every day, the load of ejaculations grew bigger and bigger. By the end of the month, things were getting pretty hot and heavy between the boys and girls. We were neck and neck, eye to eye. One day they would be on top and the next day we would change positions. The other second grade class? They were amateurs. With them, it was all for play. We, on the other hand, were on a mission.

We didn't even stop for recess. One of the things that you had to do to make the ejaculation count, was to bow your head each time you said the word, "Jesus." I can't imagine what the people driving by the church parking lot, which was our playground, thought when they saw thirty second graders wondering around in circles, bobbing their heads up and down while counting on their fingers. Most of the kids said the words to themselves. Others, were quite vocal, almost screaming, "Oh, suffering Jesus! Oh, sorrowful Mary!" They acted so holy, but most of us thought they were just faking it. Towards the end of the month, the boys gave it one last push and came out on top.

The climax of the whole event was when Sister Mary Alice came into our class to congratulate our class for winning. After looking at her sister, Sister Mary Jane, she reminded us about the sin of pride and that our true joy should be about how much suffering we had saved the poor souls in purgatory. She said God must be very proud of us and that the poor souls who were now in heaven must be very grateful and happy. I was happy. The contest was a good break from the hell I was going through trying to get through every day of school.

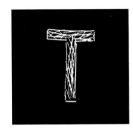o me, every word had multiple meanings. Everything was open to interpretation. I had a hard time trying to figure out which one of the infinite number of answers was the one this world, this Church, this school and Sister Mary Jane wanted. After the ejaculation contest, she actually thanked me for organizing the boys. Then she said, for the first time, the phrase that I would hear from every teacher for the rest of my life as a student. She said, "Jerry, you are clearly smart. I just don't know why you do so poorly with your school work. You just must not be trying hard enough." I didn't know either, but it sure wasn't because I wasn't trying.

One afternoon we were given a bit of busy work. We got one of those sheets of mimeographed paper, the kind that smelled so good when it was hot off the printer. I recognized that it was one of the same printouts I had seen in first grade. The page was divided into squares and each square had a letter of the alphabet. The assignment was to draw a picture of something that began with each letter. I didn't draw an apple to go with "A". I thought that was too obvious and that it would show that I wasn't thinking. I drew the idea "after." I illustrated an elaborate drawing of a book falling off a desk and a man looking behind himself at the book. In a cartoon balloon over his head was the same scene with the book resting on the table. Then I refined the letter with filigree and laced the line around the square with vines. By the time I had filled in the details, the rest of the class was finished with the test. I thought that

I would at least get an "A" for effort. Instead, the teacher sent me home with the paper, a big "F", and a note saying that I couldn't come back to school until my parents came for a conference about their problem child.

My father took off work. It was a very big deal. I was scared to death. I was confronted with the test and told, "Why don't you try harder? You can't make it in this world if you only know how to draw. You have to learn how to read." When I was asked, "What do you have to say for yourself?" Feeling like a zero, I answered, "Nothing."

They sent me to the back of the room while they talked among themselves about what to do with me. I couldn't hear what they were saying. I was too busy listening to the voices in my head. The voices that were once so loving had started to become mean. My parents and the nun called me back to the front of the room. My father spoke for the group. This father of eight children with three more still to come, said to me, the fifth born, "We hate to do this, but you brought it on yourself. So, from now on, until you learn to read, we forbid you to draw. If we catch you drawing, you will be punished. We are doing this for your own good. Someday, when you are older, you will thank us."

I was shattered. The one thing that set me apart, that made me whole, was taken away from me. Why was I being punished? I wasn't sure if this was purgatory or if I had entered some kind of hell that would last forever and ever. Was I being punished by the Roman God for not believing in Him? It certainly seemed like my own God had deserted me. What could possibly be the reason for me to have been born?

On the way home, my father told me the origin of the phrase that described being insane, "Sitting around all day cutting out polka dots." The reason we lived in Colorado was because my father moved to the high, dry climate from Kentucky because he had Tuberculosis. He was in a sanitarium that also had a "crazy" wing. There was a brother and sister there who sat in a room, "happy as clams," all day cutting out polka dots. He said he didn't want me to end up in a place like that. This was the first piece of good news I had all day. There was a place for people like me. I sat alone in the back seat of the car, hoping that I didn't have to wait until I was grown up before I could go to the safety of an insane asylum.

For a while, I went underground. I drew out in the chicken house and in the process, learned a very important thing about art. I couldn't share my drawings with anyone. The chickens just weren't interested. I learned that, for me, sharing the experience and the inspiration is an integral part of what the art is all about. The art, itself, is just a device to help communicate a state of being. My life is less about the art than what the art is about. The art isn't about answering a question.

It is just a way to frame the question so that the viewer can come up with their own answers, their own questions. Life is personal. Everyone can, and should, see it in their own way. When I began to see that my world was being drawn from my own lines of thought, life itself, became the ultimate creative act. Of course, I didn't read this situation this way while it was going on. I was too disconnected to make those kind of connections.

I buried the part of myself that drew, until I was forty years old. It took me thirty years before I started to let go of the resentment and hurt that stuck me to this point in my past. It took me that long to own it. It was, simply, too hard to hold. Every time I tried to look back at my childhood, I only saw how I had gotten burned. I gave up drawing, but I always remained an artist of some sort. In high school I wrote poetry and was the president of the drama club. In my early twenties I became a photographer. When I began to draw again, I began with a ruler, a template of circles, a sheet of scratch-board and a scratch pen. The scratch-board is solid black. The light lines are revealed by scraping away the darkness. Some of these

drawings are in this book. From my first set of scratches, I made a tarot deck of personal impressions that have made a difference in my life. Each one contains an optical illusion. The simplest one is "Focus." The four vertical lines are perfectly straight. Focusing can be a good thing and it is important to recognize another part of its nature. I noticed when I focus on only one thing, by definition, I had to unfocus everything else. I've discovered, on more than one occasion, that my single-mindedness has distorted my perception and left me susceptible to becoming blind-sided from something outside my field of view. When I thought of my self in only one way, I was condemned to play the same movie over and over again.

I've come to understand that "suffering for my art" and even the term "artist" are beliefs that don't serve the artist or the art. These ideas separate us from one another and from our own, naturally, creative selves. As Eric Gill once said, "An artist is not a different kind of person. Every person is a different kind of artist." Once, at one of my photo exhibits, I told that quote to a man who had said, "I'm no artist, but you, you are an artist." After I told him the quote, he added, "That's all very nice, but I still am no artist." I asked his wife, who was standing with us, "What does this guy do?" She answered, "He's a brain surgeon." I couldn't help but laugh, and then I added, "Okay, let's see? What do you do? You take tools and skillfully alter a medium. You look at what is in front of you and you make decisions about what belongs and sculpt away the rest. Then you take another tool and carefully, artfully, do your best to do as beautiful a job as you can? How is that any different than doing what an artist does?" "Okay," he answered, "maybe so. I'll think about it."

How we think is how we create our greatest work of art, our own life. We were born to create. It is our most natural and dominate activity. As a child, our insatiable curiosity spawned and fostered the creativity we needed to create an entire language, as well as a way to make sense of every physical object, color and concept that our new world offered. Unlike the way adults perceived reality, every object was an experience, not just an object. A ball was round and felt a certain way in your hand. It smelled and tasted like something when you put it in your mouth. It bounced or it didn't bounce, it rolled, it was a certain color when it was in the sun and a different color when it was in the shade. It was, like everything, infinite and infinitely fascinating. It was fun to learn. To learn was a form of creation. Something that didn't exist, once it became known, became real. The experience was akin to what our state of being was like before we were born. To create is Divine.

When I started to draw again, the drawings had a cartoonish, "a second grader could draw that" feel to them. I rather like that.

Being a kid wasn't all bad. I still found solace looking at the world of nature. I still enjoyed playing with my brothers and sisters and my classmates. But even that had become half-hearted. There was always a voice telling me that I should be studying. Always a voice asking what is wrong with me. Always a voice that wondered if I would be better off dead.

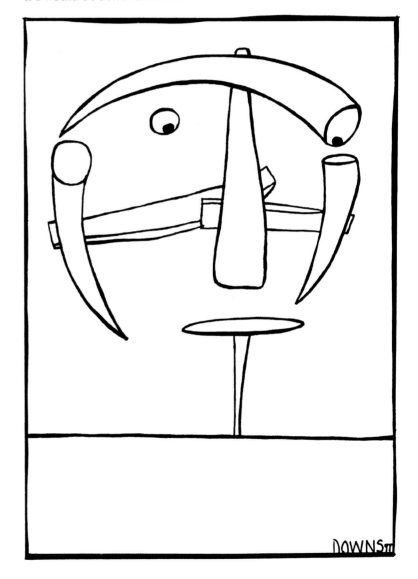

If you are going through hell, keep going.

—WINSTON CHURCHILL

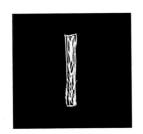was lucky. Every few years, I was given a reminder in the form of a near death experience that helped put things in perspective. They were events that asked me straight out, "Do you want to be here?" When I was in eighth grade I had an event that scared the hell out of me. It was Fall. School had already begun. When we got up in the morning it was cold and we all wore sweaters and coats to school. By the time we were out of school, every one was in shirtsleeves, dragging our coats and sweaters behind us on the way home. We, meaning my father, turned the pilot light off on the furnace every Spring to save money on gas. In the Fall, when it got cold during the day, we would turn it back on. This year, when even a sweater wasn't enough to keep you warm during the day, it was my turn to light the pilot. I had seen it done a number of times.

It was really very simple. First you got out a thin metal rod that was about 2 feet long that rested all year on a nail next to the furnace. The alligator clip had broken off the end that was used to hold a match, so the match was held on with a rubber band. After you get that in place, you lit the match and guided it through the machine and put it above the pilot light burner. Then you turn the gas knob and held down a spring loaded button for a few minutes and let go. I did all those things, except that I did them in the wrong order. I held in the button that was releasing the gas for a couple of minutes and then lit the match.

It's difficult to tell, in a timely fashion, what happened next. It was not just in slow motion. It was outside of time. First, I saw my whole life, every instant of my thirteen years, pass before my eyes. It's hard to put into words. It didn't happen in words. It was more like a chemical reaction. No, it was more like an emotion. It was as if each memory had been ignited and each glowed to life all at once. They weren't seen or felt individually. Every moment from the day I was born until I lit the match, matched one another in significance. It was over the same instant it began.

My first thought was that this must mean that I was dead. That's what happens when you die, right? Then my years of Catholic training kicked in. I thought to my self, 'Fuck. I wonder if that Playboy I looked at last week,' the one I stole from the drugstore, 'was a mortal sin.' 'Oh Jesus,' I continued, 'Oh Jesus. Oh fuck. I am so fucked. 'No, no, I don't mean 'fuck.' The focus of my attention turned heavenly, 'Jesus, I'm sorry I said "Jesus!" I'm sorry I said "Fuck! I'm sorry I looked at the Playboy.' I was bartering, begging big time. I asked all the saints I knew and Mother Mary, too, to intercede for me. Hell, believe it or not, I even called up those poor souls whose ass I helped to get out of purgatory, for help. I had just seen myself bobbing my head up and down on the school parking lot, an instant before.

I didn't see St. Peter. I didn't see God. It was at the exact moment, just as I thought I might spend the rest of eternity burning in hell, that I saw a bright glowing light. I saw a wall of flames engulf me. Then, knowing for once and for all what my fate was to be, with absolutely nothing left to loose, I spoke the one word that best expressed my feelings at the moment: "Fuck!"

The blast pushed me through the air and into a wall that was about eight feet away. Thank God, the blast also released my finger from the gas feed.

This was one of the most profound religious experiences of my life. I literally had the hell scared out of me. I wasn't afraid of burning in hell. I wasn't afraid of dying. I wasn't afraid of God. I wanted to be alive. I had gotten my reminder and I was good to go for a few

> The Eskimos have fifty-two names for snow because it was important to them:
> there ought to be as many for love.
>
> —MARGARET ATWOOD

more years. Another one happened when I was 16.

I was driving with 4 of my high school friends. We were on our way to a mall. On this particular day, the radio was blasting just like normal, we were heading down the same road we normally took, then I felt my arms, completely independent to my thoughts, turn the steering wheel and make a hard right at the exact moment a speeding car ran the stop sign and just before it would have hit us if we had gone straight. Everyone in the car got thrown around. We all turned around and watched the other car speed down the hill. My friends thought it was a miracle. I knew it for the miracle it was. It, once again, straightened me out for a few years. As always, after being lost in bad grades and the overwhelm of being someone who walked around with the mantra of, "What's wrong with me?", I, again forgot.

Not one of these events ever caused me any real physical damage. All that happened when the furnace blew up was that it "sun" burned all of my exposed skin and singed off my crew cut hair, my eyebrows and eyelashes.

Not all of these reminders came in the form a death defying feat. Some were moments of extreme beauty. Ned, one of my high school friends, who is still my friend today, and I double dated one night. When we went into the movie is was bitterly cold and had already snowed a few inches, the kind of snow that is so cold, so dry, that it is impossible to pack it into a snowball. It just falls apart in your hands like dust. By the time we left the movie it had snowed three more inches and the sky was beginning to clear. Ned and I looked at each other and knew, tonight was going to be the night.

It looked like the stars, moon and planets had all aligned to grant us our wish. We had a plan. We would take our girlfriends out into the country and take them down a deserted dirt country road that ran along the mountain foothills. When we saw the faint glow of the moon rising we knew, if we were going to make it, we better get going. We jumped in the car, my family's station wagon, the kind of car before there were bucket seats, just two long couches, one in front of the other. We told our girlfriends, Renee, who was sitting next to me with my arm around her and Sherry, Ned's girlfriend, with his arm around her in the backseat, that we wanted to show them one of the most beautiful things that they had ever seen in their lives. It was a surprise, a gift, a prize and a present. And we added, laughing to ourselves, that we were going to give it to them over and over again.

Our timing couldn't have been more perfect. I pulled onto the road and went to the place Ned and I had staked out the night before. The full moon was rising over one of the lowest hills that undulated up and down on this stretch of the country road. There wasn't a single track on the blanket of powder snow. I turned off the lights. Millions of the billions of snowflakes sparkled in the moonlight, each one mimicking a star in the now clear sky, overhead. It was hard to say what was more beautiful, the stars, the rising moon, the sparkling snow or the look on Renee and Sherry's faces. I kept an eye on the moon until it was time for me to say, "That moon rise was great. Now, let's watch it set." I left the lights off and slowly drove the car forward. Soon the moon was setting behind the next higher hill. I slowly moved forward again, stopped and we all watched the moon rise again on the other side of the hill. We did it again and again. We watched the moon rise and set and rise and set and rise and set and rise again. It was more than we had dreamed of and everything we had promised.

We were ecstatic. We all jumped out of the car and danced around in the middle of the road like little kids. We tossed handfuls of snow at one another. The kind of snow that sparkles like stars in the moonlight and falls to earth before ever reaching the laughing face of the intended target. We let the heat of the moment carry us until we were positively freezing. Ned held Sherry. I held Renee and we all looked at the moon one more time before we ran back to the car that was still running and still blasting out heat on the highest setting. We got back in the car and began to warm one another's hands, one another's frozen lips. We stayed until the heat had to be turned down because we were all so hot. We stayed until the stars, the moon, the snow and the earth disappeared as we disappeared into one another behind the steam soaked windows.

All this happened before we began to have "actual" sex. This gave me something to look forward to, something to live for. After I dropped everyone off I drove home reliving the night, playing the movie over and over again in my mind. When I got to our driveway I turned off the lights, turned off the car and coasted in hoping the crunch of the snow beneath the wheels wouldn't wake my parents. The next day was Sunday. It was the usual scene. Someone ironing a shirt. Someone looking for a pair of socks. Someone polishing the shoes. And, my father screaming, "God damn it, we've got to go!" We had to get to church early enough so that we could all be in the front pew.

When I was talking with my, now adult, sister Mary, about this, she said, "Sounds just like Mommy. Always trying to make us look like the perfect holy family." I'm sure there was some of that but, it actually had a more pragmatic purpose. In those days, Catholics received Holy Communion kneeling down. So, we wanted to be the first pew to file out to get the host that had been transformed into the body of Christ. If we weren't in the front pew, than who ever was would see the entire line of our large family and they would see the bottom of our holey shoes. When everyone was in the car that Sunday morning when I was 17, after my blissful night in the moonlight, I looked up as my father started to drive out the driveway and the sun caught the windshield. The inside of the glass, in various positions, were the impressions of dozens of naked footprints. I wanted to die.

My father said to me, sitting in the backseat with one of the little kids piled on my lap, "Clean that up when we get home." He never said another word. He had a hard time talking about sex.

When I was in sixth grade he took me pheasant hunting. We drove for hours, almost all the way to the Nebraska border. We never even saw a pheasant. I took a shot at a rabbit, but missed it by a mile. I was glad. I had learned my lesson earlier about watching something die when I was in third grade. In the back of a Boy's Life Magazine was an ad for the Northwest School of Taxidermy in Omaha, Nebraska. My parents knew that I loved animals and thought that this might be a good profession for me. The thought that I might grow up to be an artist scared them. They said they would pay for

the lessons. I signed up. They sent me the first lesson. I caught a starling in a leg trap. Another animal had gotten to it by the time I found it, but I still dissected it according to the directions. It was only a starling, the ugliest of birds, but upon close examination I could see the prismatic colors in the black feathers. I could see beneath those feathers were muscles, a body, a heart. I saw its beauty.

The lessons kept coming. I kept getting further behind. My parents kept paying. I set more traps. I caught a skunk. This wasn't good. No animal had gotten to it. No animal would have dared. It was alive, very trapped and very unhappy. I felt terrible. It's leg was clearly broken. I had to kill it. I though about killing it with an arrow. I was a pretty good shot, but I wasn't looking just to kill it. I wanted to kill the idea of ever having to kill something again. I wanted to kill being a taxidermist. I got a shovel. As I approached, it began to spray me. I hit it as hard as I could, it sprayed me some more. He gave me all he had and I, once more, gave it all I had and he went limp. I buried him/her (males and females look the same, you know) right on the spot along with the leg trap. Perhaps you have smelled a skunk run over on the road. It's strong. But when it is up close it is almost unbearable and it burns. It's a kind of acid and the acid was so thick that it was dripping off my skin. My eyes burned. It was hard to breathe. I deserved it. I accepted the smell, the pain as my penance for my sin.

So, I didn't mind not hitting the rabbit. It wasn't until the long ride home that night that my father approached the subject of sex. It was painful to watch. He began, "Ah, you like animals, right?" "Yes, yes I do." I answered knowing where he was going. "Well, pheasants, they are sure pretty birds." He paused. "They are. They really are." To give him an opening I added, "Even the hens are pretty in their own way." "Exactly!" he said with great relief. Now the ball was rolling. He thought for the next mile or two about what to say next. I imagined that he was considering that he still had another fifty miles to spit it out. I waited and ate a Hershey Bar. I asked him if he wanted any. He took a bite. I'm sure he would have rather had a shot of bourbon. He continued, almost, no not almost, exactly, like he had been rehearsing the words for the last bit of eternity. He said, without interruption, "Well you know how, like you said, there are cock pheasants and hen pheasants. Well, they have those beautiful feathers because of these things called genes and the genes, well the genes, the genes have to get together and you know how the hen has

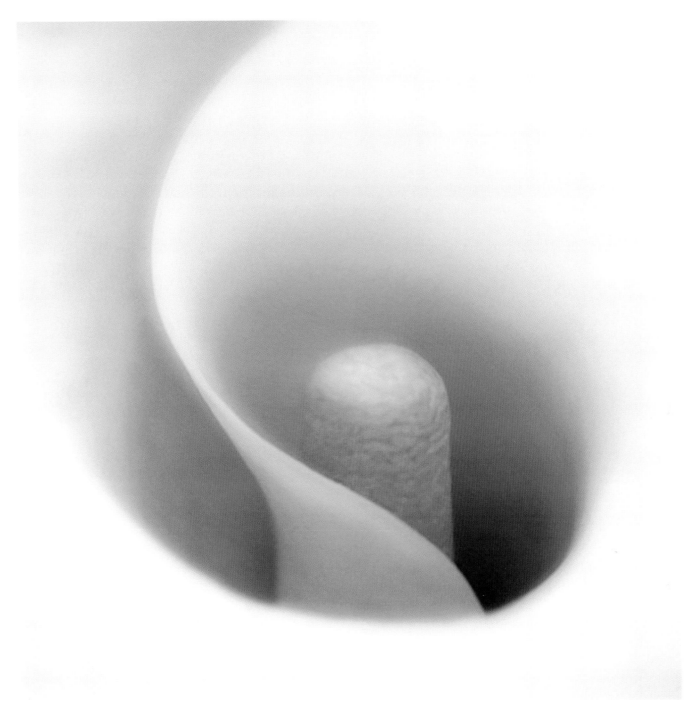

Sex is nature, and I believe in going along with nature.

—MARILYN MONROE

an egg and you know how they hatch and and and," his voice trailed off as if he had forgotten what came next or if that was all that he had come up with. I looked at him. The poor guy, this father of eleven kids, was absolutely scared stiff. I couldn't take it any longer. I had to put him out of his misery. I said, "If you are talking about sex. I know all about it. I learned it in school." After looking to the sky and saying a silent, "Thank you God.", he said to me. "Okay, then good. Well, if you ever have any questions, don't be afraid to come and ask me."

That was the same thing my mother said, one night when I came home late from a date. There was no coasting silently into the driveway and slipping into the house. The porch light was on. That meant only one thing: one of my parents was up waiting. I walked to the door and was greeted by my mother holding a rosary in one hand and a small aperitif glass in the other. I faced her straight on as soon as I remembered that my underpants were sticking out of my back pocket. I tucked them in as she said what she always said to all of us, "Where have you been? Do you know what time it is? I didn't know if you were alive or dead. Get in here before your father wakes up."

That part was normal. The part that wasn't normal was that she had been drinking. She and my father always had a cocktail when he got home from work, but drinking wasn't a big part of what went on in our house. She asked me to sit down. She wasn't drunk, but the inhibition destroying aspect of the drug had taken full effect. She said, "You know about sex, right? Well, it is a sacred, beautiful thing." "Yes, yes it is a very beautiful thing. Absolutely divine." I answered, truthfully. This was my mother talking. The same woman who would tear the bra ads out of the Ladies Home Journal so the boys in the family wouldn't have impure thoughts. She hid them under the her mattress to keep them in case she wanted to read the articles that were on the back of the censored pages. I, personally, took this as a great act of kindness. There was this great stack of super soft porn that, when each page was laid one after the other, took up the entire surface of the bed. She continued, "I just don't understand what is going on in the world. If you have sex before you are married, why should you bother to get married?" "That's a

good question." I again answered truthfully. Then added, "for love." so that she wouldn't think I was just being a smart ass.

Then she said what she hadn't been rehearsing for me, but something she had been telling herself for a long time, "I love your father. You know we have sex. That's how we had you and all the other kids." I kept my mouth shut. She resumed, "Your father loves to have sex. I like it too. It is something we share. We can't, I'm mean, we don't want to have birth control. The Church says it is not God's will." I thought I knew what was coming next. Something about getting someone pregnant and how I had to be careful or better yet, not do it at all, as she and my father did, until I was married. I was wrong. She said, "Being pregnant is our form of birth control." I, truthfully, had nothing to say, nothing I could say. Though it hadn't been invented yet, the phrase entered my mind, 'That is way too much information.' Then she wrapped it all up with, "Your father knows about sex. If you ever have any questions, don't be afraid to ask him." I said I would, kissed her good night and sent her to bed.

This was my mother talking, whose own mother died when she was 10 years old. She described the day she died as, "The happiest day of my life." Her mother was very abusive and would do things like cut my mother's eyelashes off because she didn't want her pretty little girl to become vain. My father's father died when my father was 6 years old. They both had a lot of issues about their childhood and having 11 children was the way they chose to work them out. They wanted to make the lives of their children better than the lives they had as children. They did. They, like everyone else on the planet, did the best they could, given where they were coming from and by believing the beliefs that helped hold them together.

They, just like every priest, nun, rabbi, imam, shaman and new age guru, are all just trying to come up with a way to hold the miraculous and monumental fact that we exist. It took me a while to let them be just who they are, each a different expression of the Divine. It took me a while to remember the epiphany I had in second grade, the thing I tried to share with Sister Mary Jane, "God is everywhere. God is even in our confusion." It took me a while to understand relativity. It took a while for me to see how we relate and how we, and everything in the universe, are all related.

If I ever conceive any original idea, it will be because I have been abnormally prone to confuse ideas...
and have thus found remote analogies and relations which others have not considered.
Others rarely make these confusions, and proceed by precise analysis.

—Kenneth J.W. Craik, physiologist, 1943

When my son, Christopher, was little, we drove to Goshen, Indiana to see his grandparents, my wife's parents. She would fly and the two of us would drive through the cold Midwest and play games to keep one another entertained. We played the alphabet game. We would take turns naming different kinds of animals. I would say, "Ant." He would say "Armadillo." Back and forth we would go, anchovy, arctic fox, aardvark, antelope, anaconda. We both loved and knew a lot about animals. Whoever was the last one to say a name would get the point. If either one of us could come up with the name of an animal that had some reference to the environment, we would get additional points.

So, say we were on "S" and we saw an American flag, we could get points if we said, starfish or stripped bass. The more obscure the better. We both had to agree on how many extra points the connection was worth. The starfish would have been a "4" and the stripped bass would be a "7."

Somewhere in the middle of Nebraska, Christopher, who was on the letter, "C," excitedly exclaimed "Chicken! and it's a 10 synchronicity, too!"

A "10!?" I questioned.

"Yes, absolutely! Just go back. I'll show you." he demanded. I paused, lost for a moment in being an adult. We were making good time and I wasn't keen on wanting to go back.

"Please Daddy. It's really there." Then he played the guarantee card, "I want to take a picture." He said, knowing that we both had the license to stop anytime we wanted to get a picture. "It's just like my monster and me. Really. Go back and I'll show you." he pleaded. I turned around. This I had to see. We crossed the road to get to the other side where the chicken stood. I still didn't get it.

"Tell me." I requested. "Look at the monster I just drew. The page is mostly red and white, just like the chicken and I'm wearing

red and white. And look, if you put your hand on the fire coming out of the monster's mouth, this part at the end is just like the red part of the chicken's red comb at the end. Now, do you see!?", he said pleased with his proof.

"Anything else?" I said, marveling at the connections he was making.

"I like it. I like the monster, the fire, the chicken, the red thing on his head, my fire red sweater and me. We all go together.", he stated proudly and added," That counts too. Doesn't it?"

"Yes!" I agreed. "That is the best reason of all. You got it. This is definitely a "10!"

Christopher set up the shot. He told me what he wanted. He moved into position, drew the monster to himself, held his hand over the fire and smiled.

"Okay, I got it. Now let's get going. I bet I get the next one before you do.", I bandied him.

"Oh, yeah? You see how good I am." he crowed. We were making good time.

ynchronicities were a way that my larger self reminded me that there was, indeed, something larger than myself. They were, I might add, a much more playful way than the near-death experiences I needed to get my attention when I was younger. Instead of being the butt of a joke, I began to feel like I was being let in on the joke. The coincidences became a way to dance with the world, a way of feeling my connection.

These coincidences happened so often that one day, as I was driving home on a country road, I had the idea that I would create a book with one hundred and one (I had to include 0. It's my favorite number.) coincidences captured live on film. Each image would have be a photograph good enough to stand on its own. And just for an added little twist the photograph had to contain a number from zero to one hundred to go on each page of the book.

As I was coming up with the idea for this impossible project an Eagles song was playing on the car radio. I remember hearing them sing, "Put me on a highway, show me a sign and take it to the limit one more time." As I rose over a hill an 84 Lumber sign appeared about a quarter of a mile away. I was so impressed with myself that I slowed to a stop to discover what was sure to be page eighty-four in my soon to be best seller.

I had my cameras with me. I had the right film and my tripod. The sign was perfectly lit by the sun that had just broken through the scattered clouds. Behind the sign, the sky was almost black in the shadow of a cloud large enough to cover the sun. Everything was perfect. I was not impressed. I tried every lens and trick at my disposal, but couldn't see anything that Christopher would even rate as a "1." No matter how I tried, all I could come up with was a great picture of an 84 Lumber sign. No magic. No sacred synchronicity.

I got back in the car. Turned on the radio. Some commercial was selling something. I felt the magic disappear as I signaled, stepped on the gas and was back on the highway. I had to get where I was going but I had a hard time letting this opportunity go. It was just so good! As the sign approached, I frantically searched the sky and landscape for anything that held a connection and could hold its own as a photograph. I thought, 'wasn't the song a sign.'

I told myself that I would keep looking until I passed the sign. I passed the sign. Looking over my shoulder the sign was no longer lit and the number 84 was barely visible. It all disappeared and I let it go. A half a mile later, it hit me. I felt like I had just caught myself in a mirror that I didn't know was there. It looked and felt real, it was just all backward.

I turned the car around and headed back towards the sign. I don't remember what was on the radio. I wasn't thinking about anything except what I had learned about the thousands of synchronicities that had gone before. I remembered that you can't just make a coincidence happen. This act demands nothing less than everything. It requires nothing but going with the flow. It is a kind of cooperation, a kind of dance. Taking pictures and doing art had taught me that the more sides of a situation I could see the more connections I was able to make. The more the possibilities open up the more the connections reveal themselves. As I got out of the car about 50 yards from the sign, I thought how all of what I was telling myself sounded like an ancient Zen riddle or a bunch of New Age hooey. I let that go and looked for the arrow to show me a sign.

The sun that so perfectly lit the sign from the other side now blinded me. I moved forward to see if something would reveal itself in silhouette. To find the spot, without hurting my eyes, I looked at the sign's shadow on the ground. I moved my camera to the spot on the ground that was created by the shadow of the circular part of the sign that held the number 84. I set up my tripod so that the camera's shadow was dead center in the circle. I looked through the lens and the sun and the sign disappeared. Only the bright light of the sun and the outline of the sign remained. I looked through the viewfinder and I began to let my eyes adjust to the extreme points of view. Soon I saw the arrow, the number 84 and, to my surprise and delight, the cloud that perfectly mimicked the arrow on the sign. I set the aperture and clicked the shutter. In the next two hundred and fiftieth of a second, billions of light particles hit billions of silver atoms and exploded into craters that varied in size depending on the intensity and duration of the impact. I was, once again, connected to this and every other world. I was present and most grateful for the gift.

That was more then 30 years ago. I'm more than half way to getting all of the photos with a number in the picture and I have just as many synchronicities that don't have a number.

Someday I will be able to put the numbered and unnumbered ones together. The connections are infinite.

I've got the zero.

I've got a zebra. But I'm not sure where it is in the line up.

This proud "Portrait of the Artist" on a pier will, I'm sure, appear on the perfect page.

This one, to be sure, is a shoe in for number 5.

I'm still looking for the image that will go with this crescent moon that I shot over the only building in Crescent City, Utah.

But I do have an appealing peeling poster that uses sex appeal to promote a product to prevent peeling that I shot in the 1970s that could be positioned next to the one that I shot in 2007 that promotes the same practice and has a perfect number "40" on the speed limit sign.

This shot that I took in Hollywood in 1987 (with the "1" hour parking sign) has a number of synchronicities. Bullwinkle is holding Rocky in one outstretched hand that matches the waiter on the sign pouring wine on a platter of his outstretched hand on Bullwinkle's other outstretched hand. Across the street is a billboard advertising the movie, Roxanne, that has an image of Steve Martin in the same pose as Bullwinkle in front of a picture of Daryl Hanna.

Seventeen years later, in 2004, I met Daryl Hanna when I was taking pictures at an organic food convention. Daryl Hanna was one of the guest at a dinner. On the table, in front of each person there was a brochure that featured shots I had taken. I asked her if she would be kind enough to pose with one of the pictures of a woman dairy farmer. I knew the woman would get a kick out of receiving it. Ms. Hanna graciously agreed and, without any prompting, placed the picture on her outstretched hand. I felt like giving her an Oscar. Some synchronicities only take a second, others take their own sweet time.

I've often wondered about the mechanics of this magic. Do they just appear because I think life is funny and they appear because I like to laugh? Or, as they did when I was younger and thought life was terrible, do they appear because I need to be brought back to my senses? I wondered for example, how something like this could happen: One day I was in an art store and I saw a cartoon under the glass by the register. The cartoon was of a rabbit casting a shadow of a hand. It was so clever that it made quite an impression on me. I took a picture to look up more work by the artist, John O'Brien. Then I let it go and went about my business. Then, a couple of hours later, while I was out driving around doing errands, I came across a sign of a person casting a shadow of a rabbit. It was as if I had been dreaming in the background the whole time and the dream took note of the above normal energy of my impression, stored the energy and then searched the rest of the dream world for things of a similar frequency. It kept going and going and going until it gathered enough energy to re-imagine itself, again, in my waking state. It had taken a different form, due to the influence of what it had gathered from the mass dream of humanity and God knows what else, but there was no mistaking the connection.

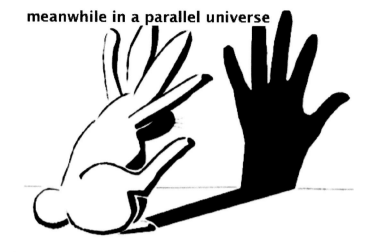

meanwhile in a parallel universe

If I included every synchronicity that happened while I was writing this book, it would have been twice as big. Here's one that hopped its way into my world:

After I had written the first draft of this book, I sent it to several friends. My friend Katherine Treffinger, graciously offered to help edit. She had sent me the revisions up to the Daryl Hanna hands. The next morning, as she reached this page, she sent me a Facebook message with this image that had been copied from John O'Brians original cartoon and this note, "I saw this yesterday. It was the first time I had seen it and guess what I read this morning?" The fact that this happened on St. Patrick's Day and that John's last name is O'Brian and he also plays Irish music sessions at the Irish Times pub in Philly, were worthy of note, but only a few points. That it showed up right then, just as she was about to read about the rabbit, with the tagline, "meanwhile in a parallel universe," I think even Christopher would agree that she deserves a high 5 and a solid 10 points!

I don't think I will ever know the exact mechanism of this magic. I kind of like that. I like knowing that I don't have to know everything. I don't even have to believe everything I think. Having been quite the thinker my whole life, I can see that my thoughts are just pillars to support my current beliefs and a way to bridge the gap between the infinite number of conflicting beliefs that I use to hold it all together. I enjoy not having to have to know it all. It keeps me going.

caricature of Trick Dick himself.

Believe it or not, I hadn't yet learned that being right didn't make everything right. I didn't understand relativity. I didn't understand Einstein when he said, "Everything is energy and that's all there is to it. Match the frequency of the reality you want, and you cannot help but get that reality. It can be no other way. This is not philosophy, this is physics." It took me a while to see that fighting against war only made more hatred, more war. I didn't see that if I really wanted to be at peace with myself, I couldn't fight against my demons. I had to make peace with them. I had to learn to stop thinking of them as "them" and realize that they were me.

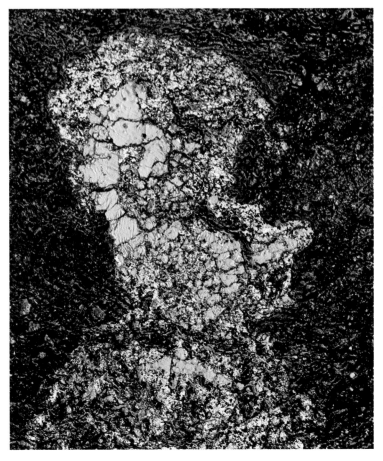

Going through all these shots in my synchronicity series I can see that some of these images were drawn to me by the thoughts that I used to hold in my head. This shot of me with another not all together billboard was taken somewhere in the Midwest when I was in my early 20s. Now I can see how, energetically, I was still plugged into resolving issues from my childhood, still trying to get myself together, spiritually, in a way that fit the bill. Bored and disillusioned, I was still playing with my personal demons and illusions. Though, I must admit, this picture still puts a smile on my face.

In the early 1970s, a few weeks after I came up with the idea for the numbered synchronicity series, I had the idea to make an even harder challenge for myself. I had a number of images that looked like human faces and I thought it would be fun to take pictures of objects that looked like every president. I dismissed the idea almost immediately. First off, I didn't even know what most of them looked like and, secondly, I couldn't see how I could possibly ever come up with an image for the current president, one whom I hated most vehemently, Richard Nixon. I hated him because of the Viet Nam War, which killed so many of my generation and my brother, Johnny. I hadn't yet put it together how I, as an individual, or a country as a whole, could create a leader to embody our unresolved issues about ourselves. Less than a half an hour later, in the parking lot outside a hardware store, I saw this

> The situation of the soul in contemplation is something like the situation of Adam and Eve in paradise. Everything is yours, but on one infinitely important condition: that it is all given. There is nothing that you can claim, nothing that you can demand, nothing that you can take. And as soon as you try to take something as if it were your own you lose your Eden.
>
> — THOMAS MERTON

A NEW YORK MINUTE

 was used to getting up before dawn to see the world in the best possible light. This day, however, I was warned that it wasn't such a great idea to go out that early, by myself, in New York City, in 1975. I was told to stay away from Times Square and, whatever I did, not to go near Central Park. I told my protectors, "Hey, it's my last day here and I can't waste it sitting in a hotel room. And besides," my 24 year old voice added something about what I had read somewhere, "I will be fine if I just think fine thoughts." To which they replied, "You can think what you want, but if you go into the park, it just might, actually, be your last day in New York or anywhere else." When I left in the morn-

ing they were all sound asleep, dreaming. I was off to take a dream shot to show the folks back in Colorado.

Being a country boy at heart, I walked out of the glass and steel canyons and headed for the trees and open meadows of Central Park. I moved from one picture to the next, excited to be in this exotic land with air so thick it almost seemed to have a color. If this was the forbidden fruit, I wanted nothing more than to take and savor every bite of this delicious, beautiful, big apple.

Satiated and satisfied with my finds I found my way to the edge of the park. I didn't know if I could take any more when, suddenly, I was asked to witness one more miracle before leaving this Eden. A black couple, who clearly had been out all night, lay sleeping on a concrete bench that bordered the park. The beauty of the yin of the round swirl of the woman cradled in the angular yang of the man, actually startled me.

It was all I could do to set up the tripod, change lenses and frame this remarkably intimate scene. It was pure grace. I felt blessed and an enormous sense of gratitude to be standing there. I was, also, full of myself. The image was exactly what I had in mind when I set out on my path that morning. I was about to bring back proof that creating reality with my own thoughts was really true. I was already starting a dialogue in my head to share with the non-believers back in the hotel. It was true. I was correct. It was also true that I had a subplot running in those powerful thoughts as I walked out the hotel door that morning. It read like some tale from the Far East, as seen in every kung fu movie, about facing one's fears, taking on demons, becoming the demons and, as a result, becoming more of yourself. I had seen no demons. I simply had allowed the magic to unfold and this was my reward.

I took my time setting up the shot. I was lost in the view that appeared in my viewfinder. Just as I clicked the shutter, I heard someone screaming, "Hey, you!" I looked up and saw three black youths running towards me at full speed. Each was larger than the next and all were larger than me. I saw them assess the scene, scanning from me to the camera to the sleeping couple and back to the camera and the frozen white guy. The leader of the fearsome trio stopped and delivered his opening line, "What the fuck do you think you're doing?"

My next thought was, in the next New York minute, I would see my whole life pass before me and it would include being arrogant to my friends who were now safe and sound asleep back in the hotel room.

It only took a second to run through my options. I considered grabbing the camera and tripod and running. They were much too

close for that. I considered using the tripod as a weapon. Even if I wanted to, there was no way I was going to take out all three of them. I was no Bruce Lee. I considered leaving my valuable camera and tripod and taking off, hoping they would think chasing me wasn't worth the effort. I considered it until I remembered the last frame in the camera.

Then, just as he was about to speak again, I, in an Aikido move that amazes me still, raised one finger to my lips and said, "Shush," and pointed another to the sleeping couple. I stepped away from the camera and whispered an answer to his question. "I was taking a picture of one of most beautiful things I have ever seen in my life." I took another step away from the camera and gestured for him to take a look. His two followers looked at him, ready to follow his lead. He looked at the couple and back at me. I took a further step away from the camera and, looking at him directly in the eye, motioned with my head back to the camera. I bowed my eyes and waited. He turned his back to me, lowered his head and looked through the viewfinder.

He was in there a while. When he was finished, he stood up, looked me right in the eye and said, "You're right. It really is." He gestured to the others to take a look. They each took a turn. He turned to me, nodded his head in recognition and then the three of them quietly walked away through the thick New York air. I took one final look through the camera. The beautiful couple hadn't changed. I, certainly, had. I wasn't so full of myself. I was more.

The original reason for art is the sacred—to be a portal, an access point for the sacred. When you see it or experience it, you experience yourself. In it you see yourself reflected. In true art, the formless is shining through the form. Ultimately, it is not everybody's purpose to create works of art. It is much more important for you to become a work of art. Your whole life, your very being, becomes transparent so that the formless can shine through. That happens when you are no longer totally identified with the world of form.

—ECKHART TOLLE

his collage was going to be the cover of my first book. It was one of the pieces that I pieced together when I was living alone in the mountains in Colorado after I lost everything and was cutting wood to stay warm. It was one of the works that I, looking back at it now, did to feed my self-worth, to convince myself that I was working. It wasn't all I was doing. I also collected, took apart and sorted the pages of thousands of magazines for fodder for future collages. I had help. I had an "in" at the Boulder Library. She would call me whenever anyone, usually an older couple, brought in their prized collection of National Geographic Magazines. The library, of course, had their own, but my friend, Karen, couldn't stand to break their hearts by turning them away. She graciously accepted them and then called me.

The library was also the source of the hundreds of videos that I played in the background while I ripped apart more than forty feet, over 20 issues of every issue of more than 20 years worth of the yellow bound beauties. For months all I did was rip and sort while I listened and looked at every sort of video they had on science, physics, nature, religion, history and psychology.

I learned a lot about the world by looking at millions of pictures and by reading the captions that accompany them. I say millions because I once measured how many magazine sheets were in an inch and then measured how many feet of paper I had sorted into boxes and the total was more than a million pieces of paper. When I went to create The Present cover collage I had plenty of images in the file of cartoons where at least one of the characters was facing backwards. I know, it sounds insane. And yet, it was just the therapy and schooling I needed to bring me to where I am today.

I learned a lot of information. I even began to understand a few things. I saw that I, like all of us, was, literally, made for this world. Our bodies are perfectly designed to operate and thrive within a certain bandwidth. We are vibrational beings. We do not perceive solid reality. We interpret waves. If our hearing was much more defined, we could hear molecules colliding in the air. Our touch can detect a vibration with a movement of only 0.02 microns (Micron = One millionth of a meter). We can follow a scent and detect its presence in one part per million molecules. Our good taste allows us the spice of life with an infinite number of flavorful combinations and our eyes can detect ten million different shades of color. Yet, every vibration that we see, hear, touch, smell and taste, all of it, is less than five percent of what we know exists in the known physical universe. If we didn't have this limitation, if we weren't dialed into this particular bandwidth, we would never be able to make sense of it all.

We know these facts because we, as a species, have come up with the devices to measure these wavelengths. Modern science set out to discover an exact model of the universe and the mechanism that makes it work. Mathematician, biologist, science historian, Jacob Bronowski, once said, "One aim of the physical sciences has been to give us an exact picture of the world. One achievement of physics in the twentieth century has been to prove that aim is unattainable." Quantum physics destroyed everything that we thought that mattered about matter. But that doesn't matter. We now just have a different model. It's just like the time when people had to let go of believing that the world was flat. The world was never flat. The world was never solid. It was just our perception that made us believe it. In both cases, it was our inquisitive nature, our spirit, our wonder, that has given us a new view of the world. Looking back at the The

Present cover collage, looking at all those backs and knowing how many other images I had to go through to find them, I see that I, like science, had to look at it all in minute detail before I came to the same conclusion: There is, in fact, no exact picture of the world.

One of the things that you can say about God, Spirit, The Creator, Being, The Divine, Science or whatever the hell or in heaven's name, you want to call it, is that It loves diversity. There are 400,000 known species of beetles and the estimates of the total number of varieties range from 1 to a 100 million. In our own 100,000 light year wide galaxy there the 200-400 billion stars. There are at least that same number or more of entirely different galaxies in the universe. We know of a single cluster of galaxies that stretches 4 billion light years from one end to the other! IT, whatever you want to call it, is interested in seeing itself manifest in an infinite number of ways. Forgetting we are a part of it all is an essential part of the Divine plan to make that possible. It is the nature of creation, itself. Creation is taking what doesn't exist and brings it into being. This applies to making a new relationship with another person, making a painting or a planet. This is what every beetle did when it found a way to thrive on eating dung or dandelions. It's all It. It's all Divine.

It's all Infinite. This forgetting/remembering, not knowing/creating, is the mechanism that drives it all forward. It is what makes IT infinite. Time, itself, is relative. The Creation of the Universe didn't happen at the Big Bang. It is happening at this very instant and we are an instrument of the Creation. We all play a part by adding our own fine tune to this masterpiece.

Reading what I just wrote reminded me of why I am pleased that the first version of The Present was never published. It went on like this for days. As Einstein pointed out, "It would be possible to describe everything scientifically, but it would make no sense; it would be without meaning, as if you described a Beethoven symphony as a variation of wave pressure." "Imagination" Einstein stated, "is more important than knowledge."

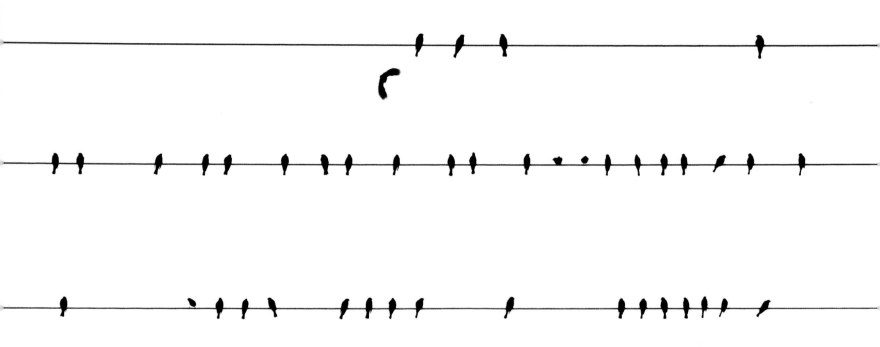

> What's beautiful in science is the same thing that is beautiful in Beethoven.
>
> There's a fog of events and suddenly you see connection.
>
> It....connects things that were always in you that were never put together before.
>
> —VICTOR WEISSKOPF, PHYSICIST

nformation, by itself, is pretty lifeless. Measurements of microns and stars numbering in the millions are mind numbing. It was only when I began to experience the implications of all the information that I had filed away in my brain did I find a way to bring it to life. I had to feel it in my body and witness it in my own life, before I could say that I understood the magnitude of what I had learned. For memorizing facts and figures, the brain is a most valuable tool, but understanding doesn't happen until we know it by heart.

I get it now. I can see why it was important to forget what we knew as a children, what we knew before we were born. If we weren't able to forget our connection we would never be able to make the connection on our own and there would be nothing new under the sun. If we knew it all, there would be no reason to know anything. Uncertainty and chaos are the nursery for every new thought as well as every star. We did it because we are the eyes, nose, and voice of the Universe. We have hands so the Universe can have a way to hold Itself and have a way to keep in touch with It's own creation. Our senses are the way the Universe makes sense of Itself. Every separation defines a new connection. Every border, between people, nations, the past and the future, separates us, and, it also defines where we touch.

If we want the world to be wonderful we have to be full of wonder. And, the truth is, even wonder doesn't last. Repetition habituates it into known knowledge and we are off on to discovering something new. It is another part of the Divine design for self discovery. When I was a child, living in the country on a dirt road, a car coming by at night was a big event. I would run into the large family room and turn off all the lights. Then I would sit on the couch and watch the light move around the walls of the room as the car passed.

When I was in my early 20's, just as it was getting dark, I was hurriedly running down a narrow stair case to get to a movie. The walls began to move. It startled me and threw me off balance. It only took me a second to realize that it was the light from a passing car projecting the pattern of the lace curtain at the bottom of the stairs. I dismissed the light moving across the walls. I had identified what it was. It wasn't a threat. There was no reason for me give it a second thought. I was, after all, on my way to see a brand new movie.

Before I reached the door I had remembered and relived my childhood memory of watching the light move around my darkened living room. I stopped, went back up the stairs and waited for the next car. When it came a minute later, I excitedly watched the pattern being projected on the white walls. It was, at that moment, one of the most beautiful things I had ever seen. Not simply because of how it looked, but because of what it made me remember. I don't remember what movie I saw that night, but I will always remember the scene of me sitting on the stairs having the flash of understanding that it's not important to walk around in awe all the time, that it's just nice to remember, every once in a while, that I have the choice, the option, to remember the magnitude of the miracle of being alive.

 ike many of us, I spend much of my day and night in front of a computer. Most days, I take a break and go for a walk. Though it, sometimes, takes me a lot to get out the door, it's always a relief to hear it close behind me. My big camera stays at home. I use the camera in my iPhone to take note of what wonders await me. No matter how many times I walk the same streets, I'm always surprised by what I see. Perhaps it is different every time, because I, myself, am a different person than the one who walked out the door the last time. Once, across from the post office, a shadow that caught my eye as it greets me with a joyous "hello." It doesn't take long before I shake the box that I'm in, tip it on its side and see what comes out. Things that I have never imagined pop into my head and I remember things that I have long forgotten. I imagine that where I am walking, dinosaurs once walked and I remember that the planet that I am walking on was once the stuff of stars. When I get home, I'm always happy that I did what it took to get out the door. It helps me get the big picture.

Across the street from the Post Office

50 feet from my front door.

Next to the barber shop.

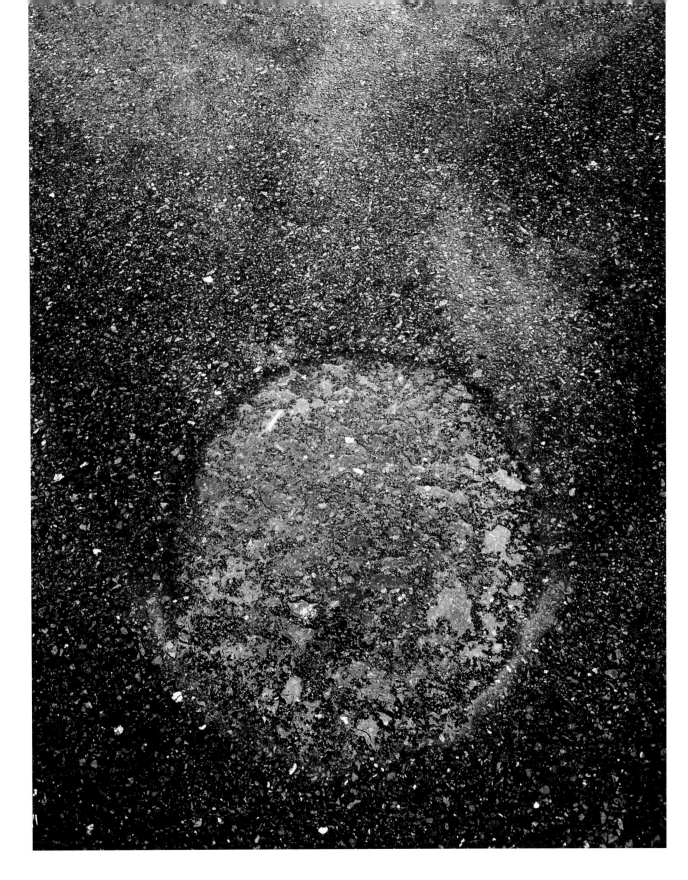

Oil stain on the street, 3 blocks away.

The present state of theoretical physics implies that empty space has all the energy and that matter is a slight increase of that energy and therefore matter is like a small ripple on this tremendous ocean of energy, having some relative stability and being manifest. Therefore my suggestion is that this implicate order implies a reality immensely beyond what we call matter. Matter itself is merely a ripple in this background.

—DAVID BOHM, PHYSICIST

The so-called physical world and so-called human body are a single process, differentiated only as the heart from the lungs or the head from the feet. You yourself are the eternal energy which appears as this universe. You didn't come into this world. You came out of it, like a wave from the ocean.

—ALAN WATTS

o see the world requires a limitation of perception. It requires an illusion. The illusion is nearly perfect. It is like a mirror. It reproduces an exact image of our reflection, and yet we have it all backwards. It's not that something happens and then we have a thought about it. We have thoughts about things and then they happen. To think that my thoughts, the way that I looked at the world, had something do with how the world looked was, simultaneously, both the best and worse news in the world. Discovering that this is all an illusion can be quite unsettling or an absolute revelation of our true selves. It can forever destroy the idea of being grounded in reality, and it can also help give us our sea legs so we can ride and even direct the wave.

Physicists and spiritual teachers have long described this reality as an illusion. For a long time I was confused and even resented that some force was purposely fooling me. As I began to play with the illusion I came to see that I was only fooling myself. This illusion is not not-real, it is, in fact, the mechanism that makes reality real. How else could you make something from nothing? How miraculous!

When you change the way you look at things, the things you look at change.

—MAX PLANCK,
PHYSICIST AND ORIGINATOR OF
QUANTUM THEORY

THE EYE IS BLIND

The eye is blind to what the mind can't see. When we look at the shadows in this picture they appear to be staggered in a checkered pattern. If you place the edge of a piece of paper on any shadow, it's clear that they are perfectly straight. Of course they are. They are the shadows of the very straight blinds. But, in this case, even logic doesn't help. Even with the piece of paper, laying on the image, proving the shadow lines are straight, the illusion persist. This is a good thing. These limits of perception are what allow us to see anything at all. It's equally good that within every limit there are still an infinite number of possibilities.

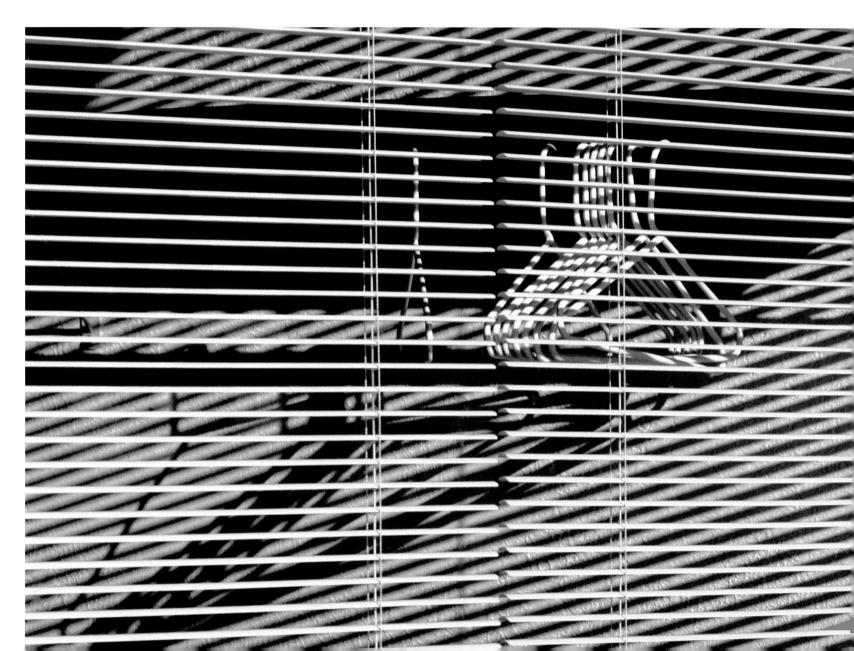

A FOREST FOR THE TREES

In this image it's hard to see the forest for the tree in the foreground. Our brain is being given all the right clues to not see what we are looking at. For starters, the image is in focus from front to back. A camera can accomplish this feat, but not our own sight. Our visual system is so efficient at focusing on where we send our attention that the illusion of continuous focus is nearly perfect.

With the same efficiency, our brain assembles an image based on our own history and visual queues. We know that the trees behind the one in front are about the same size and that the ones in the distance appear to be smaller. This perspective allows us to create a very usable sense of depth perception.

In this case, that same perspective creates a tree where there is none. The treasure of this illusion is found in the trunk of the tree in the foreground. Slowly, move your eye from left to right across the bark and you can see that the first tree in the background is really just a shadow falling across the trunk of the tree in the foreground.

FORMS AND FLOWERS

In many cases with the images in my optical illusion series, I did not see that they were illusions until someone pointed out to me what they saw or didn't see. I was showing my portfolio to a group of graphic designers when I pulled out this image. I was surprised that one of these visual experts, after a pause, said, "Wow. I didn't see the horse." Doubly surprised when another added, "Oh, now I see it." Out of the six people, only two saw the horse as the first object in the picture.

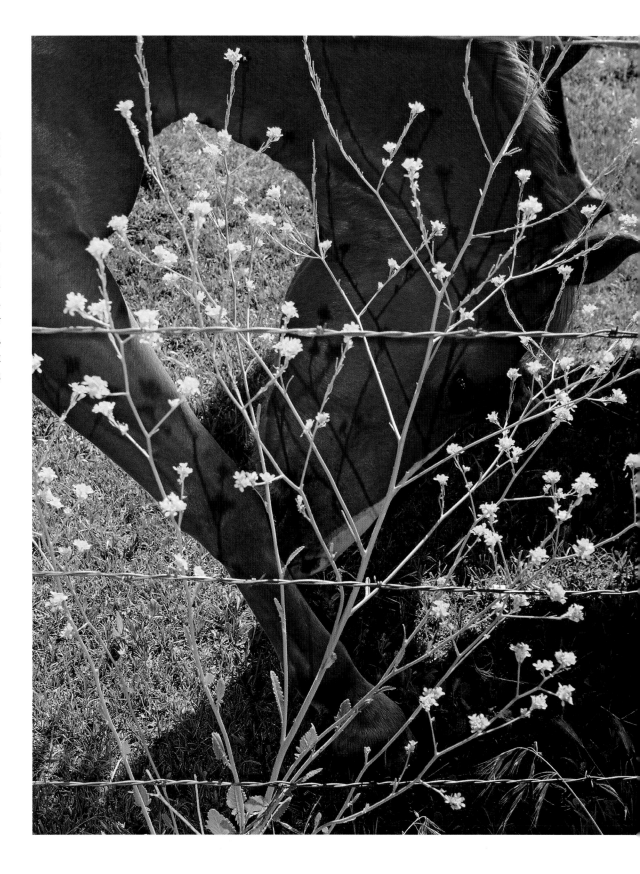

SEAHORSE SHADOW

One sunny day, I was horsing around with leaves and shadows and, to my surprise, I saw a perfectly shaped seahorse in the shadow.

DROP SHADOW

Every time I come out of an art museum the world is a different place, colors are more vivid, shapes are more pronounced. Everything seems to be alive and important. This simple elm leaf, that I found in front of the Portland Art Museum, seemed to levitate off the rain drenched sidewalk after leaving a stain and being kicked by a passerby.

FULL MOON OVER HWY.50, NEVADA

The light from a full moon illuminated the scene during this long exposure. At first glance, for most people, the RR crossing sign appears to be a telephoto shot of the moon complete with craters caused by bullet dents. Time and space, also, come into question in this photo taken outside Fallon, Nevada. I began the 10 minute exposure when the car headlights first appeared in the frame. The distance to the top of the hill is a good ten miles away. The landscape is so bright because there was, indeed, a full moon illuminating the scene, from above, out of the picture.

THE EYES HAVE IT

When I'm on a photo road trip with my friend, Joe, we only have two rules. Either one of us can stop for a picture anytime we like and we can take as long as we like to take the picture. While traveling through Idaho something caught his eye and he pulled to the side of the road. It was late in the day and I got out of the van and started to look for something to take advantage of the long shadows in the last light. After I take trips I send out an email blast and each one begins with me or my shadow saying, "Hi!" I walked over to the hay bails and while I was setting up my wave shot, I saw my shadow looking back at me. I called Joe over to give me a hand, arm and a leg to complete the face. Having friends to help you take a good look at yourself is a real service. That, my friends, is not an illusion.

A BURNING CROSS

The majority of people over 40 years old, first associate this image with a burning cross, a man on fire and a meeting of the Klu Klux Klan. Our view of the world is prejudiced by the information and images that we have stored in our head. Social and emotional reactions are stored with each piece of information and every image that we have is segregated into various parts of our brain. When we see something that triggers an emotional response we can race to a wrong conclusion. In the heat of the moment, our brains can crossfire.

Younger people who didn't live through these terrible times are more inclined to see it immediately as what it is: a burning truck. Though, I have had one 20 Something tell me that it looked like a screen capture of a video game.

WONDERLAND HILLS FIRE

To further illustrate the point that the way we perceive the world is personal, I include this image. This fire took place a couple of miles from my home when I lived in Boulder, Colorado. Hundreds of homes, including my own, received a reverse 911 call telling us to evacuate. Due to the gallant efforts of the firefighters, not a single home was lost. They were our local heroes.

At North Boulder Liquor and the local Lucky Market, I put up a poster with one of the images and made the offer to send a set of my pictures to anyone who sent me their email. Of the 186 people who responded, more than half of them thanked me for the pictures of the brave fire fighters holding fire hoses. They didn't see bystanders sitting on a fence. They saw the image that was foremost on their mind, the firefighters, the champions who saved their homes, bravely keeping the fire at bay.

Playing with illusions helped me see that I create my own picture of the world. I draw my conclusions by how I color my perceptions, my judgements. I saw that being judgmental is okay, even an essential quality to help me navigate the world. Without judgements I wouldn't even be able to tie my shoes or frame a picture. I saw that having the judgement that there is such a thing as an absolute right and wrong actually takes away the ability to make a judgement. When there is only one way to see a situation, the ability to make a judgement, a choice, has disappeared. When everything is infinite, there are an infinite number of ways to see everything.

I gave up the idea that if I just figured out how the world worked, I could simply apply the magic formula to every situation and everything would be fine. Life, it turned out, was much more dynamic, much more fluid than that. What applied to one person never applied to another in exactly the same way. Life for every person is personal. Life became a much richer place when I could make judgements and own them as my own. By being responsible for my own thoughts, I was able to respond to the world as myself.

I celebrate myself, And what I assume you shall assume,

For every atom belonging to me as much belongs to you.

—WALT WHITMAN

iven that it is all IT, I find it all pretty interesting. If you want a partner in a game of Trivial Pursuit, I'm your guy. But nothing, not the number of stars nor the dance of atoms, nothing that I know of in the known Universe, compares with the simple fact that there are other human beings. Billions of individuals just like me, each absolutely unique. Each just as complicated with their own rich history. Each of us creating our own worlds that all work together to create a larger world and a larger universe. That, astounds me!

I take pictures of people in any number of ways. Sometimes it is simply as an observer of life, like the shot on the opposite page in the Beijing Airport. The nearly black and white image symbolized for me the duality of this ancient culture speeding into the future. The hip, young woman on the left hurries behind the porter that is pushing a full cart of her luggage filled with fashions designed for her fast paced life. The older woman in more traditionally styled dress, hairstyle and shoes has secluded herself behind a wall of information stands reading a book. She is old enough to remember Mao and the chaos of the Cultural Revolution and the Great Leap Forward that destroyed millions of people, thousand of years of culture and turned China into a backward, isolated country. Both of them, like everyone in the whole world are, in our own way, adapting to the pace of the New China.

Sometimes I take pictures of people and then show them the picture and offer to email them a copy, as I did with this woman and her daughter in a photograph that was taken not fifty meters from where I took the other image in the Beijing Airport. It didn't speak

so much about China. The mother teaching her child how to play cat's cradle, spoke to me about the universal human qualities we have always shared as human beings. The feel and simple graphic quality of the scene reminded me of a painting that Norman Rockwell might have done for a cover of LOOK Magazine in the 1950s.

By far, the most enjoyable time I have taking pictures of people is when I get be with them face to face. This woman carrying her son was in a small fishing village in Southern China. She spoke no English. I spoke only a few phrases of Chinese. She understood when I used sign language by extending my open hand to her and pointing my index finger to my camera. I understood her caring for her child by the way she had surrendered her own hat to further

protect him from the heat. We both understood the universal language of a smile.

Being a photographer has given me the opportunity to see and meet a most diverse range of humankind. I've been to every state, except Maine and North Dakota and spent time in a dozen different countries around the world. There is some kind of magic associated with photography. I have asked hundreds of complete strangers if I could take their picture and almost every one has agreed. It would be completely rude to walk up to someone and ask them if you could stare at them for a few minutes, but with a camera and the right attitude it becomes a compliment, almost an honor. Perhaps they say yes to having their picture taken for the same reason I love taking their picture. I love seeing how we are connected. I push the shutter when I see that we recognize one another.

I have taken thousands of portraits of people both professionally and for my personal work. It is an intimate experience to have your picture taken. I have heard, "I hate having my picture take." more times than I care to count. Sometimes, I just laugh to set someone at ease. Other times, I take them quite seriously and comfort them until they felt comfortable. I know something that they never had reason to notice: no one can hold any feeling, be it fear or embarrassment, continuously. If someone is embarrassed they look embarrassed and then they smile or take a breath and then go back to being embarrassed or move on to another emotion. Being

a photographer gave me the license to stare at people. Through a medium telephoto lens I can see every twitch of the eye and mouth movement. If I pay attention, I can see between the breaks when they let go and show up. All I need is a split second.

There was a time when I used to have techniques, instructions, for the person having their picture taken. I would say, "Look in the lens and not at the camera. It's the difference between looking at someone's face or looking at their eyes." Often I would see a person stiffen up as they went into the pose that they had practiced in a mirror, the position they had decided was their best side and expression. They were thinking about looking good. To these individuals I would offer this tidbit, "When you are thinking about something it shows on your face." So, depending on what look we wanted to get, I would instruct, "Think about your child." or "Think about your shareholders."

I don't do that anymore. I don't think of them as "over there." If they are feeling uncomfortable, I back off and play with the camera or adjust the lights and feel my own discomfort. I let it be and let it go, then I go back to the camera and look at them as my equal, equally human, equally Divine. When I show up, they show up. When a person is perfectly present they can't help but be beautiful. For humans, it's the most attractive thing on earth. Being present is enough to delight a child or inspire the shareholders.

do a lot of work with a full range of non-profit service organizations from early childhood development to Alzheimer care. I'm honored to get to witness my fellow Beings being themselves. Most of my assignments are for some brochure or campaign to elicit funds. When I take pictures I try to show how the donor's money is successfully being used. I never try to elicit sympathy for the "under privileged." When I am introduced to people, before I take their picture, I thank them each for being a philanthropist by offer-

ing to help the organization that is helping them and lots of other people, too. This is a homeless family that came into a health clinic. The boy is simply being a kid and his mother and father are being the proud and happy parents.

I no longer make any separation between my private work and my commercial assignments. Whatever I learn doing one helps serve me to be better at the other. When I took the picture of Andrew Weil, I, after getting a perfectly pleasing shot of someone who has had his picture taken a thousand times, looked at him and said, "Okay, be you." He immediately laughed out loud. I said, "Perfect! Now laugh inside you and have it show up on your face." He knew exactly what to do. I pushed the button. He was perfectly present and I was present enough to record the gift. I never do the same

thing twice. Everyone is just too different. Being present makes it easier to see, to read, what that difference is.

Not only is everyone different, every individual has a full range of behaviors and looks depending on the emotion they are feeling at the moment. I once met this guy, we'll call him George, at a large ranch where I took pictures for a few days. A number of people told me to, "Watch out for George. He can be a real SOB." So, as I was shaking George's hand, I said, "Oh, so you're the son of a bitch I'm supposed to look out for." He looked me in the eye, while still shaking my hand with a hand that was twice as strong as my own, gave it a squeeze, laughed and said, "You got that right." We got along great. Photo instructions for George went something like, "Get your ass on the back of that truck. Look over there and act like you own the place." Of course, before complying, he always had his own retort, "Alright, get this over with. Got to warn you though, takin' my picture might just break your god damn camera."

Now, George, may in fact have been a real son of a bitch. But not all the time. Perhaps he is an SOB 90% of the time. The other 10% of the time he was a complete softy who played and acted silly with his grandchildren or had a beer with old friends or was being touched by the Divine mystery after he had pulled a calf.

I knew George had grandchildren because he had pictures of them displayed on his desk. I knew he drank beer because we each had one with our pizza that sat on the front seat of the pickup, on our way out to shoot the sunset long after everyone had already gone home on that long Summer's day. Knowing that he grew up and spent his whole life around cattle, he didn't have to tell me that sometimes he, more than once, with blood up to his elbows, had watched a wobbly legged calf stand after he had helped give it birth.

It wasn't that I was walking around like Columbo or the Mentalist, looking for clues about the person. I was just using that quality that I had as a child. The same quality that used to overwhelm me as an adult. I was just looking at everything, letting it all in and filing away what might be important and tossing out the rest. It wasn't even important to know these details. They are only good to know to get to know someone better. George, just like me or anybody else, is everything at one time or another. It's only a matter of degree which percentage of the time we spend being any one of our multiple selves. I didn't make the judgement that George was an SOB. I made the judgement that he was a good guy. I played to that part of George and that's the George that showed up.

**W**hen I am present, I show up. This, I admit, is not always the case. Once, I was having lunch in some fancy restaurant with a group of clients. I was feeling pretty full of myself and was showing off my diverse knowledge of food trivia facts. They were eating it up and kept asking for more. The table had plenty of food that provided food for thought. "The croissant gained it's name when Austrian bakers, who were up early baking bread, discovered a surprise attack by the Turks. They warned the populous and created the crescent shaped pastry to celebrate their part and to "take a bite out of Turkey", who had a crescent on their flag. The Caesar salad originated in Tijuana, Mexico, when a plane had been diverted and the restaurant where Caesar worked ran out of food for the unplanned guests. He threw together whatever they had and voilà, the Caesar salad was tossed into the menu."

I could have gone on for an hour. Our waitress arrived just as we were comparing intimate notes on the qualities of asparagus. Enlightened me, who thinks everything is equal and always likes to treat waiters and waitresses as equals, making an attempt to bring her into the conversation, just as she was topping off the water classes, asked, "How about you, when you eat asparagus, does your pee smell?"

She went limp. The nearly full pitcher of water fell onto the full glass of water and the contents of both spilled across the entire table. It was quite the scene. Everyone jumped up so they wouldn't get drenched, knocking over more glasses in the process. The waitress recoiled in horror, her eyes and mouth wide open and every eye in the restaurant was on us, on her. The manager rushed to the scene full of apologies and pleas for our forgiveness. Four more staff members arrived to lift the plates while the table cloth was replaced. The manager kindly told the waitress to wait for him in his office and, again, began to profusely apologize for all the mayhem and added that it was the waitress's first day on the job. I, immediately, as soon as he quit apologizing, told him what happened and took full responsibility, offered my own apology and asked him to please extend it to the waitress waiting in his office.

Fortunately for me, whenever I get too full of myself as a separate self, I, along with my larger Self, with my full permission and appreciation, create a situation to bring me back. When the manager heard the story, after raising his eyebrows in surprise and shock, cracked a smile and we all used the opening to relieve the built up tension and began to laugh. I mean, what else could he do? Well, the truth is, he could have done anything from laugh to get angry and throw us out. As for the waitress, who didn't make an appearance in the building while I was still present, I can't say. The range is, again, infinite. She, having been through dealing with such a ridiculous patron on her first day, could have used the event to let her know that the worst thing that could happen, just happened and become a really great waitress or it could have confirmed that being a waitress really wasn't her calling. We all, in the mythology that I currently believe to hold the most water, create our own reality and we are all in this together. The individuals at the table, everyone in the restaurant, me, the manager and the waitress all created the event. It was the same event, but each of us had our own reasons for it to manifest. Our only job is to be present, do the best we can and let the creation have a life of its own.

The petal of a flower is not more developed than the root. An ant on the ground may see that the petal is way above the root and stem, but ants are too wise to think that the petal must be better than the root.... The flower is not better than the bulb. It is not even more progressed than the bulb. It is the bulb in one of its manifestations.

—SETH/JANE ROBERTS

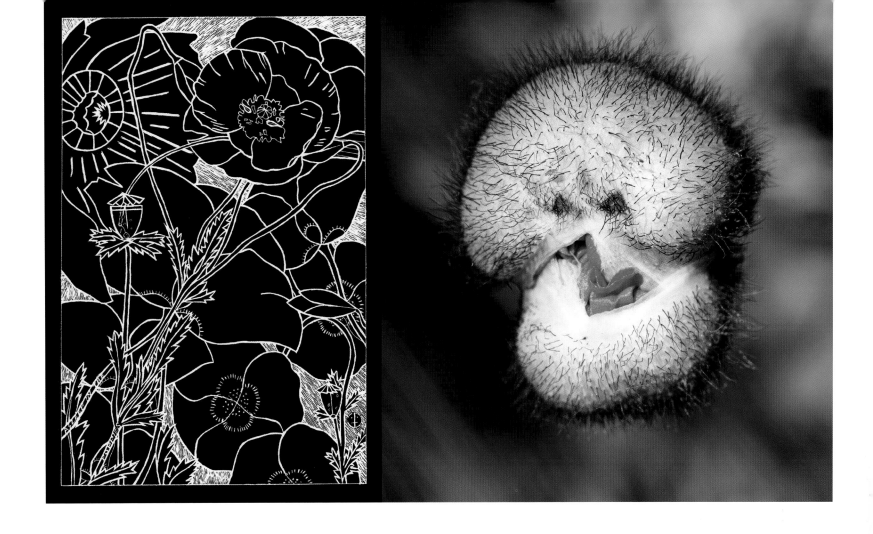

FALLING ASLEEP IN THE POPPIES

ou know that scene in the Wizard of Oz when Scarecrow, Tin Man, Cowardly Lion, Dorothy and Toto, too, fall asleep in the poppies? I know that place. I'm there right now. Metaphorically, it's that space when we can see our goal in sight and we go unconscious. All the muscles that we developed for facing the demons, witches and flying monkeys that were on our path are not the same muscles needed to hold the prize in our hands. It is a kind of death. How do I let go of what has become so familiar, for a future that I've only imagined?

I can see the book finished and I've even devised a dozen different ways to get there. I have piles of paper holding tons of thoughts and thousands of photographs in files, just begging to be used. Last week I even used having my hard drive die to slow things down. I got everything back that wasn't already backed up. I would have only had to rewrite the last ten pages. I have the notes for them, somewhere. While I was waiting for it to get fixed, time seemed to slow down when I wasn't spending all day and night at the computer. It, also, seemed to be speeding up as I calculated all the time I was loosing. Each second not writing added to the time it takes to finish the book. I even know that these symptoms are, in all probability, the side effects of Falling Asleep in the Poppies Syndrome. FAPS is not always a bad thing. Perhaps stopping to take a look is designed into the system to have us take a good look to see if the world we are about to enter is really what we wanted. After all, we made the decision to go there long before we knew what it would look like. Sometimes the decision was made when we were a little kid.

Now, I have to laugh. I just remembered the decision, the promise that I made when I was six years old. I just remembered what I forgot. I just remembered what I've been telling you throughout this whole book: Be present, do the best I can and let the creation have a life of its own. I forgot that forgetting is fundamental to the format of what it takes to get where I'm going. I just forgot that writing this book isn't just about sitting down and typing words or even having the finished book in my hands. All the experiences that I lived though, starting from before I was born, up to and including being so confused in Second Grade, a furnace blowing up in my face, making pictures, a crashed hard drive and falling asleep in the poppies are all what writing this book looks like. It's all It.

While I was waiting to remember, while I was waiting for the computer to come back, I cleaned the house and washed the dishes and all the laundry that had been piling up. I did my ironing. Yes, I, actually, iron my shirts. Even though I may wear the same shirt for days, I like starting fresh from time to time. I, also, started to go through a stack of papers that I had pulled out for possible reference material for this book. That's where I came across the quote under the poppy picture that began this chapter. It was xeroxed from the book, The "Unknown" Reality: Volume One. (A Seth Book) by Jane Roberts. Seth, speaking through Jane, was using the flower analogy to talk about how "consciousness flowers out in all directions." It

was a reference to the idea there are no levels, no sense of hierarchy, between all of our multiple selves that exist simultaneously in other realities. I still can't completely go "there" but, given the range of selves we possess right here on earth, I have some inkling of what he was talking about. Maybe, reading that sheet of paper let me pull back from my singular situation, and see what I needed to do to reconnect the larger picture. I sat down and started to write about my confusion. I started from where I was. I was confused. I did my best. I sat down and started to type. I let the creation have a life of it's own. I watched the words change the color of the white page. I listened to the words and they called to mind images that would help tell the story.

The opening poppy picture was taken six years ago on a rural road in Salem, Oregon. For 20 some years I've had the drawing of Asleep in the Poppies, that a former self, who lived in Boulder, Colorado, hand scraped out of a black sheet of scratch board on a 3x8 foot foldout table that I used as a desk in a room that I described so painfully on page 54. The picture of the poppy pod that so completely embodies that awkward and necessary stage of development that happens before we or a poppy pops into full bloom, was taken 6 months ago when I was walking around my neighborhood in San Rafael, California. The poppy on the opposite page was influenced by Asian drawings on silk, painted a thousand years ago. Now they all live in this book. The images have lives of their own and are experienced differently every time I, or anyone else, sees them. Each is a kind of portrait, symbolic of the different, multiple states of being that I, and we all, embody.

"People of Eternia! I stand before the Great Eye of the galaxy.

Chosen by destiny by the powers of Grayskull! This inevitable moment will transpire before your eyes,

even as He-Man himself bears witness to it. Now. I, Skeletor, am Master of the Universe! YES!

Yes... I feel it, the power... fills me. Yes, I feel the universe within me! I am... I am a part of the cosmos! The power

flows... Flows through me! Of what consequence are you now? This planet, these people.

They are NOTHING to me! The universe is power! Real, unstoppable POWER! and I am that force!

I am that power! KNEEL BEFORE YOUR MASTER! Fool! you are no longer my EQUAL! I am more than man!

MORE THAN LIFE! I... am... a... GOD! Now. You... will... KNEEEEEL! KNEEEEL!"

—Skeletor from "He-Man and the Masters of the Universe" animated cartoon, 1983

SPEAK OF THE DEVIL

 ne night when my son, Christopher, was six years old, he came to me in tears. Something had come to him in a dream that drove him to my arms. I rocked him back and forth the same way I had done when he was a baby.

It took time before he could voice, in words, the source of his overwhelming sadness and fear. The night before he had a baby sitter who told him that the following Spring the world was going to end. She told him that Jesus was going to come back to life and save everyone who believed in Him and that the rest of us would go to the devil. I'm sure she did it for his own good, to save such an innocent child from the fires of hell. I'm sure she wanted him to see the same light that had helped deliver her from the darkness of her own sadness and fear. I didn't push him. I knew the only thing he needed was to be held, to be connected, to know that he was not alone.

Christopher and I rocked in each other's arms. I let him lead, matching him breath for breath and sob for sob. I made comforting sounds, but no words. The movement of our bodies added a rhythm to the song that held both comfort and pain. It was a kind of dance. In time, after moving together, he gave me the lead and I could introduce a new harmony to the discord at the end of each release. Soon we were both quiet and he sat up and asked me a question that stopped me in my tracks. "Daddy," he said, "are devils real?"

I heard the sadness in his voice. I felt my own sadness that his innocence was gone. When he was four he would ask questions like, "Daddy, do real unicorns have wings?" He would be satisfied with an answer like, "Sure, if you can picture it, and you believe it, in some world it is real." I knew that the same answer was true, but that it wouldn't do much to relieve his fear. I began to dance around his question. I said, "Some people think there is a devil and a hell, but I don't."

I carried Christopher to the sink and got him a glass of water.

monsters. They are not bad. They just look the way they do because of the environment they live in. Just like the cactus that has thorns so that it won't get eaten in a world where there is not much to eat. We make up stories for things we don't understand. If we can't really look at our fears than we use our imagination to make up a way to picture them."

I knew Christopher was looking. He was asking questions. He said, "But are there things that really are bad?"

I looked at what was in front of me for another connection and said, "Well, it depends on how you look at it. It's like the guy you were named after, Saint Christopher. I don't know if he ever really existed, but the story about him is about your question. He was this great guy. He was real big and had a big heart. He, out of the goodness of his big heart, carried people across a river. But after a while he became arrogant. He thought he was a big shot. He thought he was greater than the people he helped cross the river.

One day this little boy came to the river and asked Christopher if he could carry him across. Christopher just laughed. He said that of course he could, after all, he was the strongest man in the world. He picked up the child and wadded into the river. About half way across the little boy became really heavy and Christopher began to be pulled under the water. It was like the weight of the world was on his shoulders. The little boy pulled the drowning man to the other side.

It turned out that the little boy was the Child Jesus. The Child Jesus said that he so loved and valued Christopher that he brought this hardship on him to remind him of who he was and where he came from. The hardship, the "bad" thing, came to Saint Christopher to remind him of his own love and value."

"I like that Jesus better." Christopher beamed. Then he volunteered the story of the born again baby sitter who told him everyone in the world was going to die in a few months. He asked, "How come people think that the world is going to end?"

"I don't know." I answered, "Maybe they don't like it here. Maybe they don't see this as Heaven too. Ever since Jesus died, people have been waiting for Him to return. Every couple of years, for the last two thousand years, people have been waiting on some mountain top for God to take them away. I don't think it is going to happen this time either and even if it did, who we are won't really die. I think it would be a waste of God's work and a perfectly good planet.

While he wiped the salt from his tears off his lips, I looked for a way to throw water on the devil. I remembered who I was talking to and found a connection. I said, "I think the devil is just a name we call what we are afraid of. You know, it's like animals. Some people are afraid of snakes and we know how cool snakes are. It is like the animals in the desert, like horned toads, Komoto dragons and gila

I don't know why people think the world is going to end. They see the same world we do but they look at it differently. I guess it is like looking at the stars. It can make you feel small and all alone or it can make you feel like you are connected to something really wonderful. Personally, I really like it here. I'm not waiting for God to come back. I don't think God ever left."

"But she said it was in the Bible and that God wrote the Bible." Christopher still wondered.

"Well," I hesitated, "the Bible is like every story. Every time it is retold, it changes. You can read anything into it you want. Jesus said a lot of things. He also said, 'The kingdom of God is within you.' When I read this it means that everyone is a part of God."

"Are we God?" he asked innocently.

"Yes. We are a part of God and so is everybody and everything else. God divided Itself up so that It could get a better look at Itself." I observed. "It's like you and me. We are connected and we are both ourselves. We can both help each other see different things by having two pairs of eyes."

"If God is everything, is God the devil?" he asked not so innocently.

"Well," I again hesitated. If he was older I would have quoted Joseph Campbell, who said, "My definition of a devil is a God who has not been recognized. That is to say: It is a power in you to which you have not given expression. It's pushed back. And then like all repressed energy, it builds up and becomes completely dangerous to the position you are trying to hold, and so it is a threat." Even though I always tried to talk to him like he was an adult, I knew I had to reframe the symbology. I looked at his sleeping bag on my studio floor and said, "It's like Skeletor. On one hand, he is the bad guy. On the other hand, he is kind of cool. He was made up to make the story more interesting. I mean, what would He-Man, Spiderman and every Superman, Superboy, Supergirl and Wonder Woman do if there wasn't a bad guy. They would just be Masters of the Universe in a universe that didn't need them. They wouldn't have anything to do. It would be a pretty boring story. Even those cartoons you liked when you were a little kid, like My Little Ponies and The Care Bears always had a bad guy or something that they had to face and overcome."

I paused and noticed from the look on his face, that I hadn't answered his question. I added, "Yes. The devil is a part of the whole story, but just a part. For some people he plays a big part. For others, he is no bigger than a mosquito. Everything can be good or bad, depending on your point of view. It's like. It's like. It's like what?" He really had me going now. I was at a loss for a suitable metaphor. I looked around the room. I looked out the window and saw only darkness. I was lost in space. The metaphor dawned on me just as I heard Christopher call me back to the planet, "Daddy, what is it like?"

"It's like the sun." I snapped back. "Without it we wouldn't, couldn't, even be here. It keeps us alive and gives us our bodies. It gives us the food we eat and the air we breathe. And, that is all good. But if we got too close to the sun it would be very bad. We would burn up. To us, in these bodies, the surface of the sun looks just like hell." I said, wondering if I had taken it too far and then added, "Are you ready to sleep now?"

"Almost. Will you lay down with me until I fall asleep?" He said in a voice that told me he was himself again. He had me right where he wanted.

"Sure." I laughed and turned down the light in the studio. I lay next to him, matched his breathing and wondered if he understood a single word I said or if it was just my attention that calmed him down.

"Dad!" Christopher cried out.

"What?" I answered.

"It's like the light." He stated proudly.

"What do you mean?" I wondered.

"It's like the light. You know. It's like electricity. It can kill you or it can light up the room." He enlightened me.

"Yes, exactly." I beamed.

We said, "Goodnight." Good night, indeed. I thanked God, the Devil, St. Christopher, the Baby Sitter and Skeletor. I stayed with Christopher, matching the sound and rhythm of every breath, until he fell sound asleep. Quietly, I moved away and stood silently, for the longest time, just looking at him. Quietly, I moved the umbrella light to where he was sleeping, plugged it in, attached the cord to the camera and took a picture of his angelic self.

Christopher was asleep. We had given the devil its due. I would be up for hours, doing God knows what. All was right with the world.

The miracle is not to walk on water.
The miracle is to walk on the green earth,
dwelling deeply in the present moment
and feeling truly alive.

—THICH NHAT HANH

ltimately, of course, there is no path. It's just a metaphor, a way to tour the vast expanse of the mystery. It is just a format to help us discover and expand our sense of Self. I admit, for me, this revelation, at first, brought me to a dead stop. I mean, if it is ALL IT, then what's the purpose of going on? If my love of something or someone wasn't based on how they compared to something or someone I didn't love, if all things were equal, if this was all there is, what was the point?

This way of thinking was, of course, just a conceit, a new illusion, one more marker on the path. I thought I had made sense of it, but it just didn't feel right. It took me a while before it dawned on me that how I felt was more important than what I thought. It took me even longer to realize that that was just another thought. Then, it took some time to stop making "thinking" something bad. I had to unlearn all the spiritual teachings that made the body, the brain, something to overcome before I could get to, as they variously described it: nirvana, heaven, my true self. I had to give up their path. I had to give up my path. Having come up with so many clever ways to get to it, it took a while to discover a way to, actually, hold it.

Maybe I just got tired, even bored, of seeking for a way to get it. Hell, in all honesty, I was mad that I even had to pay for it with my own blood, sweat and years.

Then something wonderful happened. It wasn't a dream. I wasn't walking in a Redwood forest. I was just walking down the street, day dreaming. I saw a thought that elicited the most marvelous feeling. I remembered myself as a little kid, with my arms extended, spinning around to make myself dizzy, just to know what it felt like. Suddenly, I was that child, laughing out loud as I fell to the ground. Resting there until the tree above me stopped spinning. I laid there and just looked at the color blue in the sky. I had to think about what I knew as a child. As a child it wasn't something that I had to think about. It wasn't something that needed to be explained. I knew it. It wasn't something that I had to earn or deserve. I owned it. Not only was it mine. It was me.

I saw how all my questions that I asked as a child were not because I didn't know the ultimate truth. They were simply questions about how that truth manifested itself on this particular planet. All of the What's this?, What's that?, How come?, and Whys, were simply being full of wonder. They were an exploration of all the things that were so clearly, so marvelously, wonderful. All the times I said, "Look, mommy, look." I was showing it to her so the Source of us both could see itself through her eyes, as well.

I saw the reason I was born and how I came to forget. My mother and father and four older brothers and sisters couldn't tell me all the answers to who, what, where, and how and when they tried, it was clear that they each had a different way of explaining the way they looked at the world. This made perfect sense. I knew that I had chosen this time and place. I chose to be born the 5th of 11 children, to grow up in the country, go to school in the city, make collages that contained thousands of different views of the same thing. It was the reason I became a photographer and a writer. I knew it was all part of my plan to see this new world from as many points of view as possible. I saw how forgetting that I was connected to everything was necessary to discover new connections, new points of view.

In the manner of a few minutes, my whole life passed before me. It wasn't like the time it passed before me when the furnace blew up. It wasn't so wildly emotionally charged. It wasn't outside of time. It just seemed to rise out of the space I was in. It wasn't neutral and it wasn't that it wasn't emotional. I was looking at it from a distance and feeling it from inside. I was filled with a great deal of appreciation and admiration. It felt like love. It felt funny. I mean, how could one person go through all of the things you just read about in this book and do it just for me, just so I could have this experience, just so I could write this book?

As I walked on, I thanked each of the selves that played such an important part. I thanked the self that chose to come here. The one who rocked the babies. I thanked the little boy who had such a hard time learning to read because he knew that words had feelings, the same one who was comforted when he found out about insane asylums because there might be a place for him. I thanked them all and all the other cast of characters who played their part. They were all a part of me. I loved them and, though it may seem odd, it took me another minute to make the connection that, if I loved them, it must mean that I loved me, too.

Why did I hesitate to make that connection? What made me, just now, hesitate to even write the words? "Before you love another, you have to love yourself." It sounds like good and sound advice when we say it to someone else but, saying "I love you" to ourselves somehow sounds conceited and arrogant.

I know the answer and I know what to do about it. The answer came to me when I was having the daydream that day as I walked down the street. I'm still working on incorporating what I heard that day into my daily life. During that minute, before making the connection, while I was thanking and loving all of my former selves, I heard my other selves thanking me for exactly the same reasons I was thanking them. I felt them loving me. I heard one of them laugh. I recognized the laugh as the same one who appeared in the dream that prompted me to do the bird collage. The one who jokingly said I needed a lot of therapy. In a voice as clear as my own, he said, "Thank you. As you love yourself, you love and honor us all. We take it as a great gift. Thank you for accepting the gift of you." He felt me hesitate at the same time I did. He added, in the same even, loving voice, with just a touch of humor, "Okay, you're a big boy now. Here's the story: You are not being conceited or arrogant if you love your gift. Who do you think gave you the gift? Not loving the gift is being conceited and arrogant. I mean, who do you think you are... God?" We both laughed. I laughed so hard it woke me up.

The daydream was over. I walked down the street. Everything seemed so real, in the same way everything can seem so real in a dream. Everything felt so connected and alive... the same way it feels when I am walking inside a Redwood forest.

When you realize how perfect everything is you will tilt your head back and laugh at the sky.

—BUDDHA

There are lovers content
with longing.
I'm not one of them.

—RUMI

ast weekend I went to a wedding reception. I rarely shoot weddings even though I greatly admire those who do. My friend Deborah was getting married. She owns a PR firm that Joe and I have been working with for years. She didn't want us to shoot the wedding. She just wanted us to, "come, have fun, have a drink, dance!" I found a photographer for her, my Facebook friend Juan Carlos. Except for Joe, Juan, Deborah, her fresh husband and her staff, I only knew a couple of the couple of hundred people attending the reception.

I, actually, love being the photographer at events. It's a blast. I can go up to anyone and take their picture, which is always an opening for intimacy. My job is to get them to smile and if I can get them to laugh, it's a piece of cake. And what's equally great is that I can leave the conversation, the laughter or the person I can't get a rise out of, anytime I like. I just lift the camera, say I have to get back to work, thank them and leave. It was odd, standing there as just myself, after meeting someone and having the same intimate and interesting conversation and not having an easy exit. Just saying, "I'm going to get a drink." seemed like such a dismissal, a kind of rejection that nullified or diminished the connection that we just shared. When I thought about it later, it occurred to me that I could have been present enough to, simply, talk about how awkward it is to end a conversion. It would be a way to acknowledge the awkwardness and a way to honor the connection we just lived through, together, for that short amount of time. I resolved to do that the next time the situation arose.

So, here I am. Given all of what we have been through, together, it feels awkward to end this book. Thank you. Sitting here, talking with you has been one of the most intimate and rewarding experiences of my life. Thank you for listening. I learned a lot about myself by having to put it into words. I, really, do think we are all connected and I can say, without hesitation, that I have heard the questions you posed and listened to the answers you offered. Again, thank you!

I'll leave you with one more drawing, one more conversation piece. When you first saw the image what did you see? Did you see the woman or a couple dancing? It is both. The woman, like all of us, has more than one way of being. Not just male and female, but, also, the child we were, the different versions of adults that we have tried on, the one of us who is completely comfortable in our own skin. We dance from one to another, in a dance that never ends. The more we know ourselves, the easier it is to dance with those selves and the easier it is to dance with another.

I love the metaphor of "the dance." I think it would be a good substitute to replace the metaphor of "the path" that we have been using in this book. It's not about seeking. It's about having.

Remember that former self, the one who worked on the collages that you see in this book, the one who kept writing after he had lost everything and was foraging for firewood to stay warm on a mountainside in Colorado? I so appreciate what he did for me, I'd like to honor him by giving him the last word:

Every moment of our lives is experienced in the present. It is like a dance. The music that moves us comes and goes a note at a time. It disappears the instant it is played and yet we find a way to keep step with what will follow. We dance for the sake of the dance, not to get done dancing. To be present, to "be here now" doesn't mean we have to eliminate our past or the future. The dance becomes beautiful, effortless, when we are able to hold our history and our hopes in the harmony that moves us all.

The hard part is already taken care of: the dance floor and the dancers have already been created. We can hold a position or we can dance. Movement makes the magic.

Let's dance!

ACKNOWLEDGEMENTS

Many people have played a part in creating this book. Fortunately, "played" has been the operative word for my most supportive friends and family. Thank you.

Joe Burull, for helping me take apart and reassemble the secrets of the universe for the last 40 years. Ned Wolf, for your support and for being an example of Being. Katherine Treffinger, the Godmother of this book, who edited and helped raise the words from mere concepts to mirror feelings with real meaning and did her best to keep me from getting too cute with double entendre and from being overly liberal with alliteration. Jennifer Downs, for remaining my good friend and giving the world our son, Christopher. Michael Signorella, whose friendship is infused in every design decision that made this book into a book.

Mommy, Daddy, Eileen, Johnny, Joey, Jimmy, (Jerry), Mary, Shawn, Maggie, Nancy, Dermod and Vincent, who chose me to be part of their remarkable family.

Dewitt Jones, James Vincent Knowles, Bettina Lindblom, Lori Fong, Jim Turrentine, Judith Carmichael, Miles Hubley, Louette Quesnoy, Bruce Fink, Connie Post, Stefan Ostman and all my photographer and artist friends for your support and inspiration. Thanks to Shannon Brunner for your playful, loving self and the playful image on page 10.

And all the following people who graciously helped Kickstart this book. Thank you all. Because of you this book is now alive in the world.

Susan Albers	Michael Braunstein	Dominique De Fazio	Denise Foxwell
Feryal Algosaibi	Lizbeth Breault	Denise De La Montanya	Jazzy Galindo
Marcella Andrews	Laurie Cameron	Stephen Dixon	Eric Gasser
Lesley Arak	Ginger Cantu	Ray Downs	Juliane Geißler
Jan Aylsworth	Bonnie Carol	Joyce Downs	Josh Gershtenson
Bill Bailey	Sharon Casey	Ward R Drennan	Leslie Getty
Jaime Barbiery	Joseph Catalano	Kevin Ebi	MaryLynn Gillaspie
Alla Barsoukova	ChaCha	Nancy Eide	Meabl Gilmore
Colette Battaglia	Joan Champ	Alicia Elliott	Laura Gilmore
Susan Bauer	Sally Chapman	Dan Ely	Julie Golden
Susanne Baum-Deierlein	David Clarkson	Robert England	Jamie Gordon
François Beaudoin	Dan Cole	José Juan Escudero	Brittney Gougeon
Robert Bellows	Austine Comarow	Jim Felt	Barbara Gritzuhn
Tim Benko	Marie Commiskey	Daniel Fick	Rob Hallifax
Ken Bernstein	Jane Cone	Shannon Fleischfresser	Sara Harris
Tree Bernstein	Edward Congdon	Chris Foley	Paul Harris
Merijane Block	Robin Crane	Michele Follger	Kara Harter
Bob Block	Russ Croop	Linda Foltz	Barbara Hartford
James Bokovoy	Danna Cuin	Ken Ford	Sean Harvey
Joan Steffend Brandmier	Nina Daye	Laura Fought	Dale Hess

Herman Hodges
Deb Hogg
June A Hood
Jan Hoyme
Tyson Hubley
Judith James
Sarjeel J Javaid
Janice L Jensen
Melinda Jones
Anne Kantola
Dee Katson
Sharon Kay
David Michael Kennedy
RoseMary King
Bonnie Kirkpatrick
Taiyo Kitagawa
Alistair Knock
James Knowles
Christine Koehler
Marina Koshelev
Carol Kovnwr
Boris Kraft
Katharina Krause-Wegmann
Kasi Krehbiel
Andrew Kubly
Gerald Kutchey
Michelle Lane
Damian Lauria
Kathleen Combs Leverett
Phil Lewis
Beau Lippman
Chhaya Loomes
Charles Lucke
Ron Lussier

Caroline MacDougall
DJ Markwell
Ruth Maruschak
Amy Matkins
Silvio Mattacchione
Susan May
Dave McAllister
Ben and Diana McBeth
Tom McGlone
Norma McGraw
Misty Mehan
Lars Ivar Mehlum
Elaine W. Miller
Bill Milner
Cassandra Mitchell
Lynda Mochan
Hyla Molander
Christiane Monarchi
Maribeth Moy
William Munder
Michael Murchison
Joyce Murton
Christopher Muscarella
Ralph Nelson
Sally Niemand
Gregg North
Courtney Novak
Kathleen O'Brien
Maria O'Reilly
Lillian Oatman
Na-Rae Ohm
Mike Osorio
Melissa Over
Mrs S. Palmer

Corena Panaccione
Tiffany Parker
Sue Parsons
Terry Pearce
Jessie Clay Pedigo
Kate Priest
Katrina Pruett
Edward Querfeld
Beryl Radcliffe
Scott Ralph
Stefan Rasch
Kathy Remener
Ted Ringer
Sam Roberts
Karynsue Rose-Thomas
Kim Ross
Jan Rostov
Karen Runge
Shannon
Margaret Scheiner
Andy Schmitt
Terry Scussel
Mary Sheehan
Madhavii Shirman
Susan Shorr
David Silver
Lisa Sinclair
Catherine Singer
Amanda Smith
Jaron Snyder
Nick Sokoloff
Eddie Soloway
Debra Soule
Jim Spadoni

Jon Spielberg
Joakim Stai
Sarah Steele
Darlene Steward
Mike Strasser
Sara Striefel
Ginny Sycuro
Margaret Sylvester
Oliver Tan
Maria Tesoro
Jenna Theiler
Lisa Thorn
Kaushik Vardharajan
Diane Vespucci
Scott Vignola
Wendy Waters
Carol Watkins
John Waugh
Robert West
RoseMary West
Clay Wilkinson
Merry Witty
Zita Xavier
David Yee
Jason Yip
Dean Zatkowsky
Helen Zawlik-Moyot
Frank Zipperer
Patricia Zoline

LOCATIONS

I'm not a serious photographer like many of my contemporaries.
That is to say, I am very serious about not being serious.

—Elliott Erwitt

About the author

Jerry Downs is an artist, photographer and writer who lives 10 miles North of the Golden Gate Bridge in San Rafael, California. His work has appeared throughout the world in books, magazines and museums. He was born the 5th of 11 children, had a horrible time in school and spent most of his life living hand to mouth trying to make a living and make sense of why he was born. Eventually he stopped trying so hard. Everything that has happened in his life has helped him understand that life is a creative act and joy is the only measure of success. He's happy to be alive and enormously appreciative that anything exists at all.